PRAYING WITH EYES
WIDE
OPEN

A Life-Changing Way to Talk with God

Sherry Harney

WITH KEVIN G. HARNEY

D0188330

BakerBooks
a division of Baker Publishing Group
Grand Rapids, Michigan

© 2017 by Sherry Harney and Kevin G. Harney

Published by Baker Books
a division of Baker Publishing Group
P.O. Box 6287, Grand Rapids, MI 49516-6287
www.bakerbooks.com

Printed in the United States of America

Library of Congress Cataloging-in-Publication Data is on file at the Library of Congress, Washington, DC.

ISBN 978-0-8010-1470-3

Scripture quotations are from the Holy Bible, New International Version®. NIV®. Copyright © 1973, 1978, 1984, 2011 by Biblica, Inc.™ Used by permission of Zondervan. All rights reserved worldwide. www.zondervan.com

17 18 19 20 21 22 23   7 6 5 4 3 2 1

"Everybody prays. Everybody struggles with prayers. Sherry gives wise guidance for the prayer-filled life."

—**John Ortberg**, senior pastor of Menlo Church; author of *All the Places to Go*

"I have known Sherry Harney for almost thirty years (we met in the church nursery!). If there is anybody who is qualified to lead us in the important subject of prayer and partnership with the Holy Spirit, it is my friend Sherry. Her spirit is so in tune with God and her pen so beautifully flows with words of inspiration. If you want to draw closer to God, put this book on the top of your list."

—**Randy Frazee**, senior minister of Oak Hills Church; author of *What Happens after You Die*

"*Praying with Eyes Wide Open* will be my new go-to book when talking to anyone about prayer. Sherry has done a marvelous job combining passionate personal experience, practical application, approachability, and biblical background. Some books excel in one; a few in two or three. I honestly don't know that I've ever come across a book that captures all four to the degree that Sherry Harney does in this excellent book."

—**Gary Thomas**, author of *Sacred Marriage*

"Sherry Harney is not just an author and speaker, she is a personal friend, the first person I think of whenever I need powerful prayer in my life. Sherry has steeped every aspect of her life in prayer and communion with Christ, and I have been blessed by her prayers for my family through the heights of joy and the darkest of life's valleys. If you want to learn to pray with fresh passion, biblical integrity, and eyes wide open to the world around you, let Sherry teach you."

—**Nabeel Qureshi**, author of *Seeking Allah, Finding Jesus* and *No God but One*

"When Sherry Harney talks about prayer, I listen—and learn! Her new book opened my eyes to fresh ways to commune with my Father. I know you'll benefit, too, from her biblical insights."

—**Lee Strobel**, author of *The Case for Christ* and *The Case for Faith*

"*Praying with Eyes Wide Open* is an invitation to experience the divine presence of God in a deeper, more intimate way. Read it to learn the unforced rhythms of doing life with God's Holy Spirit."

—**Santiago "Jimmy" Mellado**, president and CEO of Compassion International

"Simple insights are often the most revolutionary—this book has revolutionized my prayer life, through the simple invitation to pray 'with eyes wide open,' like Jesus did. Sherry smashes the shackles of popular misconceptions about prayer and sets us free into a breathtaking, biblical horizon, where we can pray at all times and in all places, attentive and attuned to the people and places around us, discovering our time with God is limitless."

—**Joshua Ryan Butler**, author of *The Skeletons in God's Closet*
and *The Pursuing God*; pastor at Imago Dei Community

"While there have been many books written on prayer down through the centuries, Sherry Harney has presented a fresh and encouraging way to pray. I have had the privilege of knowing Sherry for several years and she is one who truly lives out what she writes and teaches. She not only has a prayer life; she *lives* a life of prayer. *Praying with Eyes Wide Open* actually accomplishes several things. First of all, it gives us a practical example of how to live out the Scripture, 'to pray without ceasing.' It also helps us to be alert to see what things and people God brings into our day. Most of all, however, *Praying with Eyes Wide Open* is a beautiful invitation to *keep company with Jesus*, which is the true heart of prayer."

—**Marilyn Hontz**, author of *Listening for God* and *Shame Lifter*

"I love this book because *Praying with Eyes Wide Open* is much more than a manual on a fresh way to pray (though it is!). It is a recovery of the ancient biblical command to 'be *alert* and always keep praying' (Eph. 6:18). Sherry Harney expertly and winsomely breaks down the artificial barrier between the sacred (eyes closed) and the secular (eyes open) and shows us how to live a seamless life in which living is praying and praying is living, and Christ is all in all."

—**Ben Patterson**, campus pastor at Westmont College

"I love this book! Author Sherry Harney's book *Praying with Eyes Wide Open* helps the reader learn how to enjoy ongoing conversation with God—with eyes, ears . . . and lives wide open to Him. As I read, I found myself wanting more—more of God and the intimate prayer life that He invites us into. Thank you, Sherry, for helping me learn to enjoy a richer prayer life."

—**Nancy Grisham, PhD**, author of *Thriving: Trusting God
for Life to the Fullest*

"This book is a rare gift. Most authors can inform. Good ones can inspire. In *Praying with Eyes Wide Open*, Sherry Harney accomplishes a more challenging task: she *invites*. Each chapter is filled with a potent blend of profound reflection and practical wisdom. The combined effect for anyone who reads will be an enlarged spiritual appetite. Ultimately, Sherry helps us hear the Lord's invitation to draw near to Him with our whole self—eyes wide open."

—**Adam T. Barr**, coauthor of *Compassion without Compromise*

In the pages of this book you will meet many of my prayer mentors and heroes. Some are biblical characters, like Hannah and the apostle Paul. Others are great prayer warriors from the history of the church, like Brother Lawrence, Andrew Murray, and R. A. Torrey. Some of these people are friends and church members who have invested in my prayer life and modeled a passion for communicating with the Living God.

Among these great giants of prayer, two stand out in my life because they have spent time on their knees praying for me from the time I was in my mother's womb. Sherwin and Joan Vliem are my parents by birth and also my spiritual parents. Their authentic faith has shaped me, their trust in the Word of God has inspired me, their humility has formed me, and their prayers have covered me.

I can confidently say that my father and mother have prayed for me faithfully all the days of my life. My father has the gift of intercession. I have told my dad about needs of people he has never met and discovered decades later that he still prays for them daily. My mother has a pure faith in Jesus that trusts and believes without wavering. The two of them together have fortified me in prayer and taught me what a life guided by faith-filled prayer looks like.

I dedicate this book to Sherwin and Joan Vliem. So much of who I am, what I know, the way I love, and how I live for Jesus came from watching the two of them follow Jesus.

Contents

Contents

Section Four **PRAYING WITH LIVES WIDE OPEN**

Acknowledgments

Kevin, this book has come from my heart and life experience, but God has used your gifts as a writer to help shape my words and to make this book come alive. For your prayers, your partnership, your encouragement, and your relentless energy, I give praise to God.

Zach, Josh, and Nate, for almost three decades you have lived in a home that has been a laboratory of praying with eyes wide open. As my sons, you patiently let me pray for you countless times. Then you prayed with me through life's joys and trials. Now, you each pray for me and I am deeply grateful for the faith in Jesus and confidence in the power of prayer that we share together.

Christine, Taylor, and Brynne, you have become family, as one by one you have fallen in love with my sons. Thank you for your encouragement, your partnership in prayer, and for the blessing you have become to our family.

The congregations of Corinth Reformed Church and Shoreline Community Church have been partners in the development of this book. Each of God's people in these churches who have prayed with me and for me has been a valuable and loved partner in this project.

Marilyn Hontz, Nancy Grisham, Lee Strobel, Joshua Ryan Butler, and Adam Barr are author friends who have spoken timely words and lifted up prayers that have spurred me onward in the writing of this book. Thanks to each of you.

Lucille Patmos, Patrice Glithero, and Nancy Kreer are my mentors and mighty women of God who have fought on my behalf, laboring in prayer and lifting me up through the writing of this book.

The team at Baker Publishing has stood behind me, cheered me on, given amazing support, and trusted me with the sacred task of writing this book about fresh approaches to prayer. I am deeply grateful to Jack Kuhatschek, Chad Allen, Barb Barnes, Eileen Hanson, Erin Smith, and Patti Brinks.

The prayers of God's people ascend to the God of heaven like sweet incense. Thank you all for joining me in the privilege and delight of exalting the God who loves us and hears all we pray, with eyes closed and with eyes wide open.

Introduction

On a snowy and blustery winter day in Michigan, I took a walk with my dad. He has a daily routine of walking four to five miles each morning, rain or shine, sleet or snow. He does this right after his morning time in the Word of God and prayer. When I travel to visit my parents, I stay with them and enter into the routine and rhythm of their life. It is an absolute joy. As we neared the end of our walk on this particular winter day, knowing I would soon be heading back to my home in California, I asked if we could pray as we walked. My father gladly agreed.

As we began to pray, I was shocked when my dad bumped me into the snowbank on the edge of the road. As I fell, almost as if in slow motion, I instinctively knew what must be happening and looked back to see the vehicle I knew my dad must be saving me from. To my surprise, there were no cars on the road.

I hit the snowbank with a gentle thud, looked up at my dad, and realized what had happened. He was not saving me from a renegade car sliding toward me on the icy roads. It was something very different. Somehow, in the natural response of hearing someone say, "Let's pray," my father went into automatic prayer mode. As we began praying, he reflexively closed his eyes. This caused him to veer toward me and accidentally knock me into the snowbank.

We both laughed as he helped me up and brushed the snow off me. My dad and I ended up having a rich conversation about how, though it is appropriate to close our eyes in some situations, there are also many occasions when we are wise to keep our eyes wide open.

The next morning I received this email from him:

> Dear Sherry, I thought about you this morning while I was walking. I prayed with my eyes open. I even prayed out loud. I learned from you that if I pray with my eyes open, my time with God is limitless.

The goal of this book is to help you discover the wonder, beauty, and joy of praying through the flow of life. My passion is to see ordinary followers of Jesus grow into natural prayers who talk to God, listen to God, and interact with God at all times, in all places, through all circumstances. To do this, we will all need to learn how to pray with our eyes wide open.

Throughout this book I will use the phrase "praying with eyes wide open" in two distinct ways. Sometimes it will mean literally opening our eyes as we pray, just like I did with my father on that snowy day. When we do this, we become more aware of creation, people, beauty, and the needs around us. As we pray this way, our opportunities for prayer multiply.

"Praying with eyes wide open" is also used in a figurative sense. It encompasses praying with greater awareness of God's presence, power, and work in the world. Our eyes might be physically closed, but our awareness of God's will and desires opens us up to pray with greater passion and clarity.

Having our eyes open in both of these ways—physically and figuratively—will make our prayer life richer and more powerful.

PRAYING WITH EYES
WIDE
OPEN

Praying with eyes wide open can become a lifestyle. This means shifting our thinking about prayer and at times literally keeping our eyes open when we pray. By making this small shift, we discover that we can pray at all times and in all places. When we do this, we will find ourselves praying more.

Praying with our eyes open also allows us to see what is happening around us and engage in prayer in new ways. Rather than closing our eyes to block out the world, we open our eyes, like Jesus did. We see the need and pain as well as the beauty and joy all around us. What we see shapes our prayers.

When we pray this way, our time with God is limitless and the power of God is unleashed in surprising new ways.

One

Limitless Prayer

If I pray with my eyes wide open, my time with God is limitless.

SHERWIN VLIEM (MY DAD)

I was speaking at a women's conference in the charming coastal city of Adelaide, Australia. Just as I was about to head up to speak at the final session of this four-day event, a lovely woman came walking toward me. She seemed happy and serious at the same time. I glanced quickly at her name tag to catch her first name.

She politely asked if we could spend a few minutes talking. I was heading out to catch a plane shortly after the session and knew there could be a chance I would not have time to talk at the end of the session. My dilemma was that I normally don't engage with people's personal requests right before heading up to speak.

I quickly lifted up a brief and silent prayer with eyes wide open: "Lord, would you have me spend a few minutes with her right now, because I don't know if I will actually have time after

I speak?" I felt a gentle nudge in my heart and knew I needed to connect with her right then and there.

My natural thought was that these few precious moments were intended to serve her. To my surprise and delight, God's plan was to speak to me and encourage me through this dear woman.

She began by telling me she had had no intention of coming to the conference. A friend had invited her persistently and kindly. Over and over her friend kept challenging her to make the time to come to the conference. She found herself struggling with this decision. After going to sleep one evening, she woke up in the middle of the night and could not get back to sleep. She knew her uneasiness was about attending the conference, so she got on her computer and googled the name of the speaker: Sherry Harney. One of the things she found was a link to a message I brought to the student body of Westmont College in Santa Barbara, California. She clicked the link and watched the whole chapel message.

At that moment, she looked at me and said, "Little did I know that what I would hear in that video would change my life!"

During the message, I had spent only a few minutes talking about this idea of praying with your eyes wide open, but God had used this simple and profound idea to begin a transformation in her personal spiritual life and the lives of her children.

As she listened to the Westmont chapel message, the Holy Spirit mercifully pierced her heart. She understood, at a level deeper than she ever had before, that God is truly with her always. Her eyes were opened to the reality that she could talk with, commune with, and connect with God at any time . . . all the time. She came to see that praying with her eyes open would be necessary if she were to increase her time communing with God.

With sober eyes, this lovely woman looked at me and confessed that she was serious about her Christian faith, but she had not been communicating with God throughout her day. She had missed this great gift. Then, with an even deeper sadness, she admitted she had failed to teach her children how to pray throughout their day. Prayer had become a thing to do a certain way at a certain time, but not a spontaneous and Holy Spirit–breathed part of each moment of life. With steely-eyed conviction, she looked at me and said, "This reality broke my heart, but I determined at that moment, this will change, and I would attend the conference."

The morning after she had watched the chapel video, she got in her car to take her children to school. As they drove, this precious mom taught her children the simple lesson she had learned in the middle of the night. She explained that they could pray anytime, with their eyes open. She declared the truth that God is with them at all times and in all places. After a brief time of speaking this truth to her children, she did the wisest thing possible. She invited them to keep their eyes open, look around, and begin praying together as they traveled to school. Mother and children began to pray. They talked to God, eyes wide open, hearts engaged with their loving Creator. It felt natural and good. In the following days she continued to invite her children into this sacred rhythm of natural conversation with God.

My new friend looked at me as tears began to flow freely down her cheeks. With pure joy she told me, "Now, when we get in the car before heading off to school, my children ask, 'Mom, what are we going to pray about today?'"

She thanked me for helping her see what had eluded her for so many years. Her faith was real, she loved Jesus, she prayed often, but she had never embraced the invitation to limitless prayer. I thanked her for inspiring me and helping me see that the simple biblical truths I feel called to share with people can be radically transformational.

I asked her if I could have her name tag from the conference. I let her know that I would put it on my desk where I would be working on this book. I wanted her to know that the experience she had with her children would be an inspiration to me as I wrote . . . and that name tag has been on my desk ever since.

More than ever, I believe that lives, homes, and communities can be transformed if God's people will learn to enter into limitless prayer. When we push the walls out, break from routine repetition, and pray without ceasing, God's presence and power are released.

With Our Hands Folded and Our Eyes Closed

Think about it. When someone says, "Let's pray," what do you do? Picture it in your mind right now. Many of us will close our eyes and fold our hands. If we do open our eyes and look around during a prayer, we might even feel a little anxiety that someone will see us with our eyes open. If we lock eyes with another person who is also "peeking" during prayer, we might feel guilty and quickly close our eyes. For some reason, there is a general consensus that the proper posture of prayer is eyes closed and, more often than not, hands folded.

Here is the shocking truth. There are many and varied postures for prayer taught and modeled in the Bible. Closing our eyes is not one of them. And, just for the record, neither is folding our hands.

If we look back at practices in the ancient world, people would often avert their eyes in the presence of a king or sovereign. This might be part of the reason people have closed their eyes while praying through history. I also believe that the pattern of eyes closed and hands folded in our modern culture comes primarily from parents teaching their children to pray. If our hands are folded, we can't poke our neighbor or grab food off a dinner plate. If our eyes are closed, we can focus better and avoid the many distractions around us. These are just my personal musings, but I think, in many cases, these could be the driving forces behind this posture when we pray.

These might be helpful ideas for a child learning to pray, but we should not feel bound and compelled to always fold our hands and close our eyes when we pray. Instead, we need to learn to pray with our eyes wide open and our hands open to God and those around us.

For the sake of full disclosure, even though I have written this book titled *Praying with Eyes Wide Open*, there are times I love to pray with my eyes closed, usually early in the morning when I have to work to keep the distractions of the day's to-do list from catching my racing mind. There are times I focus better with my eyes closed. I am just offering a new paradigm, a new way to understand this amazing privilege we have all throughout our days to pray continually. Praying with eyes closed is certainly not wrong, but never praying with eyes open may keep you from living out the scriptural exhortation—and resulting blessings—of praying continually.

The Bible and Our Eyes

As I worked on this book, I read and reflected on passages throughout the Bible that speak directly or indirectly to the topic of prayer. I could not find one single passage where God calls someone to close their eyes when they pray. I did not even find a single place where the passage stated that someone closed their eyes when they prayed. I am not saying that people in the Bible or in the ancient world never closed their eyes when they prayed; what I am saying is that the Bible does not command it or even direct us to pray this way.

What we do find in the biblical text are examples of people praying with their eyes wide open. A quick survey shows this was the case in the Old and New Testaments. When Abraham's servant went to Abraham's hometown seeking a wife for Isaac, we find him standing by a spring, praying for God to make his journey successful. As he prayed, he saw Rebekah come out with a water jar on her shoulder. The passage is clear that he was praying with his eyes open, and during that prayer he saw the patriarch Isaac's future wife (Gen. 24).

When God's people were in the middle of a battle, God helped them be victorious. We read that God delivered them "because they cried out to him during the battle" (1 Chron. 5:20). It is clear that they did not fold their hands and close their eyes while in fierce hand-to-hand combat.

When Jesus lifted up what has been called his "High Priestly Prayer" in John 17, we read that "after Jesus said this, he looked toward heaven and prayed" (v. 1). The Savior's eyes were wide open when he lifted up his longest prayer in all of the four Gospels.

There is never a call or command to close our eyes when we pray, but there are examples of people who prayed with their eyes open . . . and God heard and answered these prayers.

The Bible and Our Hands

The Bible never tells us to fold our hands when we pray. But we do see people with their hands engaged, active, and lifted up in prayer. This does not mean that we must always lift our hands, but there are times this is wholly appropriate and there are many examples of this practice. Moses lifted his hands in prayer as he cried out on behalf of God's people (Exod. 9:29–33). Solomon spread out his hands toward heaven as he prayed (2 Chron. 6:12–13). David asked God that "the lifting up of [his] hands be like the evening sacrifice" (Ps. 141:2). The apostle Paul exhorted that people pray with holy hands lifted, without anger or disputing (1 Tim. 2:8). In addition, the apostles laid their hands on people as they prayed for them (Acts 6:6).

There is nothing wrong with folding our hands when we pray, but we can also lift our hands, lay them on others, and extend them to the God who loves us and rules the universe.

Sit, Stand, or Kneel

Our outward posture should reflect what is happening in our inner person as we pray. The Bible does not prescribe a set body position but a variety of physical expressions that are appropriate. Since we are called to pray at all times, it makes sense that there would not be one body position but many. King David, in a time of humbly seeking God, "*sat* before the LORD, and he said: 'Who am I, Sovereign LORD, and what is my family, that you have brought me this far?'" (2 Sam. 7:18, emphasis added). Solomon, David's son, "*stood* before the altar of the LORD in front of the whole assembly of Israel, [and] spread out his hands toward heaven" (1 Kings 8:22, emphasis added). Just a short time later we read that "when Solomon had finished all these prayers and supplications to the LORD, he rose from before the altar of the LORD, where he had been *kneeling* with his hands spread out toward heaven" (1 Kings 8:54, emphasis added). Daniel, Paul, and Jesus all knelt in prayer (Dan. 6:10; Acts 20:36; Luke 22:41). When Jesus was in the garden of Gethsemane, in the shadow of the coming crucifixion, he was on his knees in prayer, a fitting posture in a time of agony and surrender.

A life of limitless prayer will mean learning to seek the face of God and engage in conversation with our Maker as we stand, sit, kneel, run, lie down—as we are in any and every position. It is not a right posture but a right attitude that says I am always ready to pray.

Looking and Longing

One unique refrain that arose in the time of King Solomon was the call to the Israelites to turn their faces toward the temple in Jerusalem as they prayed. They were to pray toward the great city and this place where the very presence of God was said to dwell (1 Kings 8:30, 35, 38, 42, 44). They were called to look to the city and the temple as their hearts and eyes strained to see God. There is a sense that their eyes were open and looking for God.

At the same time, Solomon prayed that God's eyes would be riveted on the temple and the people who were praying. He cried out,

> May your eyes be open toward this temple night and day, this place of which you said, "My Name shall be there," so that you will hear the prayer your servant prays toward this place. Hear the supplication of your servant and of your people Israel when they pray toward this place. Hear from heaven, your dwelling place, and when you hear, forgive. (1 Kings 8:29–30)

Finally, in a massive crescendo of spiritual engagement, God appeared and spoke. He made a promise that expressed where his eyes will be:

> When Solomon had finished building the temple of the LORD and the royal palace, and had achieved all he had desired to do,

the LORD appeared to him a second time, as he had appeared to him at Gibeon. The LORD said to him: "I have heard the prayer and plea you have made before me; I have consecrated this temple, which you have built, by putting my Name there forever. My eyes and my heart will always be there." (1 Kings 9:1–3)

As the people looked toward Jerusalem, the temple, and ultimately toward God, God promised to look toward them. Not only are our eyes wide open, but God's eyes are wide open too.

When Eyes Meet

Picture your eyes meeting the eyes of God and then realizing he's always been protectively, lovingly watching you. Does this elicit a powerful sense of relationship? God's eyes are on you. In the book of Hebrews we read, "Nothing in all creation is hidden from God's sight. Everything is uncovered and laid bare before the eyes of him to whom we must give account" (4:13). God sees us at all times. He never looks away. That is one side of the relational equation. God's eyes are on us.

We are invited and encouraged to keep our eyes on God. In Psalm 123:2 we read, "As the eyes of slaves look to the hand of their master, as the eyes of a female slave look to the hand of her mistress, so our eyes look to the LORD our God, till he shows us his mercy." Our eyes should be locked on God, straining to see him in the normal flow of life. In the book of Hebrews we are challenged to "[fix] our eyes on Jesus, the pioneer and perfecter of faith" (Heb. 12:2). When our eyes are on God, and we recognize that his eyes are on us, we can communicate with him, we can talk with him—we can pray.

Praying on the Water

As I am learning to pray in all places and at all times, I have people ask me to teach them what I mean by "praying with eyes wide open." This happened with a very sweet couple named Bob and Sherry. They took Kevin and me out boating one summer evening on Lake Michigan. It was peaceful and beautiful. As we were going slowly along the lakeshore, we began talking about this book and how praying with our eyes closed is normative and almost reflexive for most Christians. They both admitted that they had never really prayed with other people with their eyes open.

As I often do, I invited them to just begin praying as we were boating, but to keep their eyes open—especially Bob since he was driving the boat! As is almost always the case, they both started out feeling a little awkward. But as they quickly began noticing the beauty of the lake, God's creation, and the magnificent setting around us, their prayers turned to thanksgiving for God's artistic beauty. Praise began to fill the air as we drank in God's glory all around us. Kevin prayed, thanking God for both Bob and Sherry, and as he prayed, he looked at each of them and made eye contact. They both made a point of not looking away. This was all new, but I could see this was strange but glorious prayer territory.

After we declared a heartfelt "Amen!" we talked about the experience. Both of them expressed delight in this new vista of prayer. It was like they had opened a window after a long winter and the fresh spring air came blowing in. I was able to encourage them to pray this way as a couple and with friends. We had experienced a sweetness of the Holy Spirit as we prayed together, with eyes wide open, making the boat ride and our time with them more special and memorable.

If you have never prayed out loud with other believers with your eyes open, I encourage you to try it. If you allow your eyes to meet another person's eyes as you pray for them, the Holy Spirit shows up and moves in a unique way. It is hard to put into words, but I have seen it happen over and over again. Praying with eyes wide open is not just about the reality that we can pray at all times. It also deepens our prayer and connects us with God and with other people on a level we might have never experienced before.

Your Prayer Journey

Over the coming week, try praying with your eyes open in another way. When you are in a group of people and someone says, "Let's pray" (it could be at a meal, at church, with friends, or some other setting), don't close your eyes. Be sure to engage fully in your heart, and join in with prayers out loud if appropriate, making a point of keeping your eyes open as you pray. Look at the person who is praying and seek to enter into prayer in a fresh, new way. If someone happens to look at you during the prayer, don't feel guilty, just smile at them and keep praying.

One little warning. You might find yourself feeling a little awkward and even guilty if your eyes are open while praying at church or over a meal with family. Just press through and notice how your prayers take on fresh, new meaning when your eyes are open.

Two

Pray Continually

I live in the spirit of prayer. I pray as I walk and when I lie
down and when I arise. And the answers are always coming.

GEORGE MÜLLER

At five years old I encountered Jesus.

I had heard about him. I had prayed to him. But on a quiet
Sunday, late in the afternoon, I laid on the sofa in our living
room and personally met the Savior.

I know, I was just a little girl, but I assure you that he entered
my life and has never left. Decades later his presence is sweeter
and his power more profound. Since that day I have grown to
love and hunger for his Word.

The Bible whispers and at times shouts the truth of heaven
when I read it. Sometimes the words of Scripture lift my spirit
and inspire me. They resonate with and penetrate my soul. At
other times the teaching of the Bible confuses me and weighs
heavy on my heart.

One such passage that troubled me for years and caused me to struggle is a seemingly simple two-word exhortation: "Pray continually" (1 Thess. 5:17). I wanted to obey God's call and follow his teaching . . . but how? How was I to pray without ceasing? How could I stay aware of God every moment and communicate my love with every breath? How could anyone measure up to this spiritual expectation?

As a young girl and later as a mom of three boys, I continued to feel this weight and pressure. I could not do it. The very idea of praying at all times, in all situations, every moment of every day, felt oppressive.

Then, after years of struggling with this passage, the Holy Spirit breathed a simple truth of understanding into my soul that changed everything. When the veil was lifted and I saw the real meaning of this passage, joy descended and prayers were expressed with a new freedom and passion. Here is what God taught me: *It is not that we **have** to pray continually; it is that we **get** to pray continually!*

This is not a simple matter of semantics. It is a spiritual reality. It is a paradigm shift of heavenly proportions. It changed everything for me, and I hope it is just as transformational for you. It is not that you and I have to pray every moment of every day. God will not be disappointed with you if you don't pray all the time. The wonder and joy is that the Maker of heaven and earth invites you and me to commune with him at all times and in all places. When we are ready to communicate with the God of eternity, his eyes, ears, and arms are always wide open.

Bigger Than Prayer

My journey of praying with eyes wide open has done more than grow my prayer life. It has transformed my understanding of

God, deepened my intimacy with my Savior, and changed the flow and texture of every day I have walked on this earth.

Prayer, in its simplest form, is about being in the presence of the God who made us and loves us. It is about relationship. When we learn to pray with our eyes wide open, we will discover in new and greater ways that we are not alone. We sense more deeply and intimately that God is with us in the depths of pain, depression, sadness, and fear. He is also present at the heights of ecstasy, joy, and delight. From the valleys to the mountaintops, God is near, his door is open, he is present. When our eyes are open as we pray, we literally see the world around us. We notice beauty, struggle, injustice, and kindness. We see God at work in the big and small things of life. All of these things move us to prayer.

When we live with an awareness of God's glorious presence in each situation and every moment of our day, prayer becomes natural. We talk with God as a friend who is walking with us through the heights and depths of this journey of life.

God's Glory and Our Good

Praying with our eyes wide open, literally and figuratively, brings glory to the God who receives eternal praise from heavenly beings who cry out:

> "Holy, holy, holy
> is the Lord God Almighty,"
> who was, and is, and is to come. (Rev. 4:8)

Acknowledging God through the rhythms of life and the flow of our day puts God in his proper place: first! When we seek to pray continually, we declare that he is Creator and we are creation, he is the Shepherd and we are sheep, he is the Potter and we are the clay. All prayer is for the glory of God.

At the same time, prayer is for our good. When we pray with eyes wide open, we grow in our awareness that God is present, powerful, and protecting. As our hearts and eyes tune in to the presence of the Living God, we discover that he delights in our desire for him. God rejoices when his children encounter him as their heavenly Father. Keeping God in the center of our attention and life-focus glorifies him and benefits us.

The great eighteenth-century revivalist and preacher Jonathan Edwards described this connection of God's glory and our good expressed through prayer with these words:

> With respect to God, prayer is but a sensible acknowledgement of our dependence on him to his glory. . . . Our prayer to God may excite in us a suitable sense and consideration of our dependence on God for the mercy we ask, and a suitable exercise of faith in God's sufficiency, that so we may be prepared to glorify his name when mercy is received.[1]

In his book *God's Passion for His Glory: Living the Vision of Jonathan Edwards,* John Piper elaborates on this idea: "Prayer is calling on God for help; so it is plain that he is gloriously resourceful and we are humbly and happily in need of grace. The Giver gets the glory. We get help. That is the story of prayer."[2]

One of the great gifts of prayer is that it does two astounding things at the same time. First and most important, it brings glory to God, who is worthy of all praise and honor. Second, and also deeply important, is that prayer gives us what we need most. It connects us to the Lover of our soul. It fuses our heart to the Father's heart. It grows our relationship with our God.

These are all good things we need. Prayer is truly for God's glory and our good.

Jesus, Our Perfect Example

Jesus is our example of all things good and beautiful. When we follow in the Savior's footsteps and watch his life story told in the Gospels, we discover that prayer saturated all he did. Jesus prayed continually as he journeyed here on earth. A brief survey will inspire us to learn to pray like our Lord and Savior.

The Savior prayed in public. With a crowd of mourners gathered at the opened tomb of Lazarus, we read that Jesus lifted his face and voice toward heaven:

> Then Jesus looked up and said, "Father, I thank you that you have heard me. I knew that you always hear me, but I said this for the benefit of the people standing here, that they may believe that you sent me."
>
> When he had said this, Jesus called in a loud voice, "Lazarus, come out!" (John 11:41–43)

Jesus also prayed in quiet and lonely places. "Very early in the morning, while it was still dark, Jesus got up, left the house and went off to a solitary place, where he prayed" (Mark 1:35). After the previous full and taxing day of ministry, teaching, and healing, Jesus felt the need to slip away to be with the Father.

Jesus prayed in the most public of settings and in quiet places as he retreated from the world and sought the face of the Father. When we pray with our eyes wide open, we too will find ourselves communing with God when we are alone and when we are surrounded by people.

When Jesus was going to make a big decision, he cried out in prayer. Choosing his followers was a critical moment in the ministry of Jesus, so he made space for prayer: "One of those days Jesus went out to a mountainside to pray, and spent the night praying to God. When morning came, he called his disciples to him and chose twelve of them, whom he also designated apostles" (Luke 6:12–13). What a beautiful model! Like Jesus, we should talk with God about every important decision before we make it.

The power of heaven moved through Jesus and he performed many miracles. A precursor to these life-changing moments was often prayer. "Taking the five loaves and the two fish and looking up to heaven, he gave thanks and broke the loaves. Then he gave them to the disciples, and the disciples gave them to the people" (Matt. 14:19). Over 5,000 men plus women and children ate this gift of bread, and there were even leftovers. Prayer marked moments when heaven intersected with earth.

Healing was often accompanied by prayer. "He looked up to heaven and with a deep sigh said to him, 'Ephphatha!' (which means 'Be opened!'). At this, the man's ears were opened, his tongue was loosened and he began to speak plainly" (Mark 7:34–35). Jesus spoke one word and the power of heaven was released.

Prayer was so important to Jesus that when a major spiritual experience was on the horizon, Jesus gathered people to pray with him.

> About eight days after Jesus said this, he took Peter, John and James with him and went up onto a mountain to pray. As he was praying, the appearance of his face changed, and his clothes became as bright as a flash of lightning. Two men, Moses and Elijah, appeared in glorious splendor, talking with Jesus. (Luke 9:28–30)

Jesus asked these three friends to pray with him in anticipation of this encounter.

As we survey the life of Jesus, we do not sense that prayer was reserved for special and sacred moments of separation from everyone and everything. Of course there were times when Jesus sought the face of the Father in private intimacy, and so should we. But the majority of Jesus' prayers are in the flow of life, in public settings, and many times lifted to heaven with eyes wide open.

How Prayer Changes an Ordinary Day

It was a last-minute flight across the country for the funeral of a dear friend. I got a ticket on Southwest Airlines and that meant I did not have a reserved seat. Southwest is unique because they do not give you a seat but a boarding group (A, B, or C) and a number. When you walk on the plane, you can take any available seat. Those who fly on this airline know the drill. If you are in group A, you are sure to get a good seat. Aisles and windows are plentiful! Group B boards next, and they tend to gobble up what is left of the window seats and a few remaining aisle seats. Those who fly Southwest regularly joke that a C on your ticket stands for "center" because there is a very good chance you will be snuggled into a center seat between a couple of people who were in the A or B boarding groups.

On this particular day, I not only had an A on my ticket for the first boarding group, but I also had a very low number, which put me at the front of the line. While waiting, I found myself excited about the fact that I would be boarding very early in the process. I was actually daydreaming about all the wonderful seating possibilities that would await me as I walked onto the plane. Do I want a window seat or an aisle? I was getting a bit giddy inside. Maybe I could even get an exit row and really stretch out.

As the array of options ran through my head (only those in the A group have the luxury to ponder such choices), the Lord gently reminded me of the prayer I had lifted up earlier that morning. I had started my day talking to God in the privacy of my bedroom. I had prayed that God would use me throughout the day, committing to serve him and others.

Now, out of nowhere, the Holy Spirit whispered into my heart this convicting question: "Sherry, is this what your life has become?" The words were not audible, but I knew what the Holy Spirit was trying to reveal. I knew the message he was speaking.

It had become all about me. I was trying to get the best seat for *me*. I said a quick prayer, with my eyes wide open, as I was walking onto the plane. "God, please don't let my life be just about me. I want what you want." It was a quick breath of a prayer. It was not complicated. I did not kneel down. I did not close my eyes.

I can't say I heard a direction for exactly what seat I should take, but I knew God was doing something. So intentionally, even though a wonderful and inviting exit seat was available, I decided to take a seat behind the exit row.

A short time later a man in his early thirties sat down in my row with me. We cordially greeted each other and then we both went about our own business. I silently prayed, "I don't know what you are doing, Lord. Maybe that stirring was just about me getting my heart right. I am here, and I am available." For the next hour we both focused on our own work.

All of a sudden we hit a dramatically turbulent patch of air and the plane dropped and rocked violently. Everyone on the plane got very quiet. I mentioned to the man next to me that I flew a lot and I had never hit air quite that rough. We both nervously chuckled about my comment and then we started chatting.

I asked what kind of business he was in. He had a very interesting job and I continued asking lots of questions because I found his work intriguing. In the process of our conversation, he shared that his mother had died a few years back and it was a very disturbing time for him. Through this loss of his mom, he also lost a lot of faith. He went on to explain that during this time of struggle, he was seeking something more, something deeper and lasting. He said he didn't have peace in his life and he was presently investigating Buddhism as a possible answer to his heart's longing.

After listening to his story, I asked if he would mind if I shared how I find peace each day. He responded by saying he would like that. I shared about how having Jesus in my life has made all the difference to me. He listened intently, and at the end of our conversation, I realized we were about to land. I asked if he would mind if I prayed for him in his search for peace. He was very open.

I told him that we did not have to close our eyes. I even explained that I would pray quietly and I would *not* be grabbing his hand. I lifted up a simple and heartfelt prayer, and when we were done, he actually grabbed my hand, squeezed it, and smiled.

I ended up getting his contact information and sent him some books. He sent me a very nice thank-you email, expressing my prayers were appreciated and uplifting.

I had started my day in a time of private prayer. Later, while in line to get on my flight, the conversation with God continued. This time it was dynamic, I was in public, and God was pushing me to check my attitude and outlook. Because of this I ended up in a seat I would not have chosen. That small shift opened the door naturally for a spiritual conversation. That led to another time of prayer, with eyes wide open, with a man who was carrying pain and loss and seeking peace that only God can give.

As my dad said, "When we pray with our eyes wide open, our time with God is limitless." Life becomes an adventure. Prayer guides us. And ordinary days and moments become extraordinary experiences saturated with the presence and power of God.

Your Prayer Journey

Over the coming week, take time every day to pray with your eyes open. Make a point of praying in situations where you would normally not be praying. Pray silently and try praying out loud (when the situation is appropriate). Take note of how you are praying more often and how prayer is moved and guided by the things God places right in front of your eyes.

Three

Relationship Matters

In simple prayer we bring ourselves before God just as we are, warts and all. Like children before a loving father, we open our hearts and make our requests.

RICHARD FOSTER

The day started like any other, but by the time I went to bed that night, I would look back and realize I had received one of the greatest gifts of my life. It was about 6:00 a.m. on September 7, and it was my thirty-fourth birthday. I was having some quiet time with God on the sofa in the living room before my three boys would wake up and bring joy, energy, and volume to our home. I heard a stirring and looked up from my Bible to see my middle son quietly trying to sneak past me. Josh, our then five-year-old, was headed to our bedroom. I found it curious that he was up this early and wondered if he had remembered it was my birthday.

I listened, trying to figure out what he might be up to. I realized he had snuck into my bedroom closet. I knew there was a box filled with cards for all occasions tucked in the corner but did not know if Josh was aware of this. I was surprised when my son appeared several minutes later with a card in one hand and a little unwrapped blue box in the other. It wasn't just any box—it was his favorite school box.

He walked over to the sofa where I was reading and quietly handed me the card and box as he said, "Happy birthday, Mom." I was amazed and deeply touched by this kind act of a little boy so early in life and so early in the morning. Even if there had been nothing in the box, the very thoughtfulness of his actions had already brought joy to my heart.

I looked at his little face and said, "Oh Josh, thank you so much."

As I opened the card, which I still have, I had to smile. Instead of addressing it to MOM, he had written the card to WOW. Josh was still working on getting his *W*s and *M*s figured out, and it was quite early in the morning. He signed the card, "I Love You." There were all sorts of cards in that box in my closet. I was pleased that he had actually found a birthday card and not pulled out a sympathy card.

As I thanked Josh for the card, he just smiled. I held the little gift box on my lap. It was covered with pictures of racing cars and classic cars. Josh sat quietly as I opened it and looked at the contents. To my surprise there were four gifts in this special school box. As I looked at them, I realized each item reflected Josh's love for me.

I took each gift out of the box and held it in my hand; I was overwhelmed by a deep sense that this was a special moment of love between a son and his mother. The first item was his favorite little Matchbox car. I turned to Josh, thanking him for such a sacrificial gift. I told him that I knew this was his favorite car, and he nodded.

The second gift was a quarter. This was all the money he had accessible to him at the time. "Josh, how special that you would give me all the money you have."

The third gift was a handheld toy that he always took with him whenever we traveled in our car. It was a little pinball game. This was before video games, cell phones, or electronic gadgets were used to entertain kids while traveling. He loved this little travel toy.

I sat there and thought to myself, *Wow, could this gift get any better! His favorite school box, all the money he had to give, his favorite Matchbox car, and his special travel toy.* You can imagine the heart of a mother receiving such a loving and sacrificial gift.

As I looked back in the box to retrieve my final item, the significance of this gift was not as obvious. I picked up the item and held it in the air so both Josh and I could see it.

It was a set of children's plastic play handcuffs.

I knew there had to be significance to this gift but was unable to come up with it, as I had with the previous three. I had worked as a second-grade schoolteacher for a few years, so I used my educational skills to unravel the mystery. Kindly, I spoke to him, "Josh, what were you thinking when you put this in my special gift box?" He spoke quietly, "Well, I was thinking since today is your birthday, maybe you could put one handcuff on one of your wrists, and I could put the other one on my wrist, and we could spend the whole day together."

Tears welled up in my eyes. "Oh Josh, thank you so much. I would love to spend the day with you." And we did!

That experience has become a picture of love that I continue to remember and share with others. In that moment, the Holy

Spirit impressed this thought on me: *You know the joy you feel right now toward your son? That's how I feel when you want to be with me, to talk with me, to encounter me.* I knew God was teaching me through Josh's gift box. I was overjoyed that my son would give with such sacrifice. I was also touched that what he wanted most was just to connect with me.

With each passing year, I learn more about prayer. This experience with my son Josh seared truth deep in my soul. Prayer is not first and foremost about making lists, getting our words exactly right, reciting memorized supplications, or using a particular posture. It is about developing a deep and vital relationship with the God who made and loves us. It is about coming to our heavenly Father and saying, "I want to be with you, all day long!" When this is our heart condition, our words become prayer and so does our silence . . . for we are connected (handcuffed, if you will) to the God who loves to be with his children.

Our Theology Impacts Our Prayer

Prayer is more about the God we pray to than the exact words we pray. When we understand this truth, when it sinks in, our prayer life is transformed. If we see God as an angry, aloof, absentee landlord who launched our small planet into space and left us to our own devices, we will not pray. Or we will only pray out of obligation or a sense of duty. Why bother? If we do bother praying to such a stern and distant deity, our prayers will be guarded and cautious at best, and fear-filled at worst.

On the other hand, if we see God as he is—deeply loving, staggering in his patience, and shocking in his forgiveness—we will run to his arms. When we see God with clear vision and eyes wide open, prayer is not a chore but a deep and natural desire. When we see God as he is, we want to be with him, we love to talk with him, we ask if we can be handcuffed to him all day long, every day. When this happens, prayer is a never-ending conversation with the one who loves us beyond description and who we love more with each passing day.

Everything about prayer hinges on what we believe about who God is. Our theology will move us to prayer or drive us away from him. We need a proper view of God, and the pictures we carry in our heart can make all the difference.

God Is Creator

Our prayers become passionate and powerful when we understand that God is not only the Creator of the universe but also our Creator. He is very personal. In Genesis we see God shaping and forming the first people and breathing life into their lungs (2:7). God's creating process was personal and intimate. In the book of Psalms, David declares, "For you created my inmost being; you knit me together in my mother's womb. I praise you because I am fearfully and wonderfully made; your works are wonderful, I know that full well" (Ps. 139:13–14). When we realize that the Creator of the heavens and earth was also intimately involved in making us, we can trust that God knows what is best for us. We will want to be near him and commune with him.

In the book of Isaiah, we hear the heart of God cry out to his people. They have wandered from his arms, forgotten how to pray, and forsaken their Maker. Instead of seeking God, they have embraced idols and acted unfaithfully. With a passionate longing to bring his people back to his loving arms, God reveals the empty vanity of idols and declares exactly who he is:

> Listen to me, you descendants of Jacob,
>   all the remnant of the people of Israel,

you whom I have upheld since your birth,
and have carried since you were born.
Even to your old age and gray hairs
I am he, I am he who will sustain you.
I have made you and I will carry you;
I will sustain you and I will rescue you. (Isa. 46:3–4)

In these two brief verses, the Creator teaches his children at least three distinct things that should inspire us to pray. *He carries us.* Idols have no life, they must be carried, and they are actually a burden to those who believe in them and must tote them around. If you read further in Isaiah 46, you will discover the clear description of not only the uselessness of idols but also the burden they cause: "They lift it to their shoulders and carry it" (v. 7). In stark contrast, our God carries us in our times of pain, loneliness, and brokenness. Like in the well-worn poem "Footprints in the Sand," when someone looks back at the hard times of their life and discovers that only one set of footprints can be seen, they might despair and think that in those moments God left them. The poem goes on to remind us that at those times, God was carrying us. This is the picture God paints in Isaiah. There are times, from our childhood and into old age, when the God who created us picks us up and carries us through the storm. We have all had moments of loss, sorrow, sickness, and pain. In those times we rightly say things like, "If God had not carried me, I would have never made it."

In this same passage in Isaiah, God assures us that *he sustains us.* These are the times we keep walking on our own two feet, but the power and presence of our Creator helps us endure the challenges and weather the storms. In these moments we don't need to be carried, but we absolutely need to be infused with his divine power and aware of his intimate presence. This empowers us to walk on and keep following him.

In addition to carrying and sustaining, God also *rescues us*. Because he made us and loves us, there are times when God simply delivers us from ourselves or the actions and harm others might bring upon us. I am convinced that on the other side of this life, we will see the countless ways God has intervened on our behalf, often without us having any idea. Of course, the greatest rescue is when Jesus died on the cross and bore our sins, shame, and the judgment we deserved. There is no greater rescue than being delivered from sin.

If we live each day with a deeply biblical and personal conviction that our Creator carries us, sustains us, and rescues us, we will be compelled to communicate with him. Prayers of praise will flow from our hearts and lips. Cries for help will be frequent, because we will know he loves to deliver us. Confession of our need and brokenness will be uttered. When our eyes are open to see the love and care of our Creator, prayer comes naturally and freely.

God Is Father

When Jesus taught his followers to pray, he addressed God with these words: "Our Father in heaven, hallowed be your name" (Matt. 6:9). Jesus himself called God *Abba*, an intimate word that means "daddy" or "father" (Mark 14:36). Then, the apostle Paul told us that we can address God using this same name, *Abba* (Rom. 8:15). In 1 John we are taught, "See what great love the Father has lavished on us, that we should be called children of God! And that is what we are!" (3:1). God is our Father, and through faith in Jesus we become his sons and daughters. What an amazing truth! If we embrace this reality and see ourselves as loved children, we will be compelled to talk with our heavenly Father.

Jesus paints a vivid picture for us of God's fatherly love and provision: "Which of you, if your son asks for bread, will give him a stone? Or if he asks for a fish, will give him a snake? If you, then, though you are evil, know how to give good gifts to your children, how much more will your Father in heaven give good gifts to those who ask him!" (Matt. 7:9–11). This comparison is intentional and compelling. Jesus wants us to realize that even though we human parents are broken by sin, we can still provide for our children and extend care and love to them. How much more will a perfect heavenly Father provide for and bless his children? The picture of a truly loving father should stir our hearts. When we recognize God as the perfect Father whom our hearts have always longed for, we pray with new confidence and trust.

Through the years I have heard people say that the image of God as a Father is not helpful for those who have been abandoned, abused, or deeply hurt by their earthly father. Some feel that speaking of God as Father can even be hurtful. I believe we need to reclaim what the world has broken. If we have a marred view of our earthly father, we need to grasp an understanding of God as a good and perfect Father even more. My heart goes out to those who have not had fathers who loved or provided for them. If that has been your experience, it is my prayer, even now as I write, that God by his Spirit will restore in your heart the right picture of your heavenly Father. You have a perfect Father in heaven who sees you as his beloved child.

Some years ago my husband, Kevin, led a team that conducted Sunday worship services in a local jail. On one of these visits, the chaplain pulled Kevin aside and reminded him that any "father" language when referring to God would not be helpful and should be avoided. It just so happened that it was Father's Day and Kevin was feeling led by the Holy Spirit to do a whole sermon about God as our perfect and loving Father.

Here was the dilemma. Would Kevin listen to the jail chaplain or the Holy Spirit? You are probably already ahead of me. Kevin boldly taught the men in the jail, in all three of the cell blocks, that they have a loving, faithful, ever-present, forgiving, powerful Father in heaven. He explained that none of us have perfect fathers, and some of us have absent or very poor earthly fathers. But the good news is that we have a Father in heaven who is perfect and we can always trust in him. That Sunday the men responded with joy, tears, and excitement. When they realized that they had a Father who knew everything about them and still loved them, they wanted to pray and talk to this Father. In all three services the men came forward in greater numbers than any other time to be prayed for.

In the same way, when we have a relationship with God, we can draw near to him with joy-filled confidence and speak to him in prayer. As his children, we can cry out, "*Abba*, Daddy!" We can tell him our joys, fears, victories, and defeats and know he cares about them all, because our heavenly Father loves his kids.

The Tender Motherly Heart of God

The Bible never uses the term "Mother" for God, and we are not called to address God as mother. But the Bible does use a number of beautiful and powerful images of God's gentle care, and some of these images reflect the tender heart of a mother. The prophet Isaiah records the heart and words of God when he writes, "As a mother comforts her child, so will I comfort you" (66:13). Earlier in Isaiah, the prophet writes, "Can a mother forget the baby at her breast and have no compassion on the child she has borne? Though she may forget, I will not forget you!" (49:15).

When Jesus laments over Jerusalem, he cries out, "Jerusalem, Jerusalem, you who kill the prophets and stone those sent to you, how often I have longed to gather your children together, as a hen gathers her chicks under her wings, and you were not willing" (Matt. 23:37). Just like a hen gathers her chicks and protects them, so God watches over us. In the book of Hosea, with sobering words, the prophet paints a picture of God disciplining the people of Israel like a bear robbed of her cubs (Hos. 13:8). As we deepen our prayer life, pictures of God's tender and loving motherly heart will draw us close in prayer.

God Is Shepherd

In the ancient world of both the Old and New Testaments, the work of a shepherd was familiar to all. Shepherds led, protected, and provided. Good shepherds loved their flock and would die for the sheep they cared for. God often presented himself as the Shepherd of his people. Isaiah writes, "He tends his flock like a shepherd: He gathers the lambs in his arms and carries them close to his heart; he gently leads those that have young" (40:11). What a picture of tender care and gentle love! This is the God we talk to every time we pray. In Psalms we are invited to worship, kneel, and engage with God as the sheep of his pasture:

> Come, let us bow down in worship,
>   let us kneel before the LORD our Maker;
> for he is our God
>   and we are the people of his pasture,
>   the flock under his care. (Ps. 95:6–7)

In one of the most loved and familiar passages in the entire Bible, the Twenty-Third Psalm, we see a powerful picture of how we can relate to God as our Shepherd. David, a man who knew a lot about shepherding, wrote these words, inspired by the Holy Spirit. Though they might be familiar, read them slowly and remember that this is the God you speak to when you pray with your eyes open or closed:

> The LORD is my shepherd, I lack nothing.
>   He makes me lie down in green pastures,
> he leads me beside quiet waters,
>   he refreshes my soul.
> He guides me along the right paths
>   for his name's sake.
> Even though I walk
>   through the darkest valley,
> I will fear no evil,
>   for you are with me;
> your rod and your staff,
>   they comfort me.
>
> You prepare a table before me
>   in the presence of my enemies.
> You anoint my head with oil;
>   my cup overflows.
> Surely your goodness and love will follow me
>   all the days of my life,
> and I will dwell in the house of the LORD
>   forever. (Ps. 23)

Kevin and I live only a couple of miles away from the Fort Ord National Monument that includes over fourteen thousand acres of hills and eighty-six miles of hiking trails that are all protected public land. We have a Saturday morning tradition, when we are not traveling, to do a six-mile hike in these hills. This has become a sacred time for several reasons. We connect and catch up as we talk with one another. We also always spend time praying for family, friends, our church, our community, and the world. We naturally pray with our eyes open and find this a refreshing time on so many levels. It is always a highlight of our week.

One other reason this weekly ritual has become special for us is that we often get a powerful reminder of God as the Good Shepherd. It just so happens that a present-day shepherd and his sheep graze these hills. They are there to keep the wild grasses down, but for us they have provided many beautiful pictures of spiritual truths.

Every time I spot the sheep, I try to find the shepherd. This is a vast area of land, but I know the shepherd is never far away. His eyes are always on his flock. Each time I scour the hills with my eyes, I find great delight and feel a sense of relief when I see the shepherd.

One day we noticed the shepherd was walking a few hundred yards ahead of us with one of his dogs. We had never seen the shepherd away from his sheep. We quickly glanced to see where the sheep were. They were quite a distance away but were being well taken care of by the other dogs.

The shepherd was clearly on a mission, and we wondered out loud, "Do you think he's looking for a lost sheep?" It didn't take long for us to notice that, to the right of us, he had suddenly found the sheep. It was lost and sick. With tears in my eyes, I watched as this shepherd used all his skills to maneuver this sick sheep in the right direction, from calling him forward to physically picking his backside up and pushing him in the right direction. It was a beautiful sight. This shepherd cared for each of his sheep. He would not let one of them go. What a great picture of a good shepherd!

When we recognize that God is our Shepherd and he provides, guides, refreshes, protects, blesses, and prepares a place for us, we are compelled to talk with this Good Shepherd. We trust at a deeper level and love with greater passion. When we encounter God as our heavenly Father, we run to his arms and call him *Abba*. When we are stunned by the reality that our Father is the Creator of the universe, we thank him for fashioning us and for being intimately involved in the smallest details of our life. A theologically solid view of God grows our relationship with him, and this in turn moves us to pray.

Your Prayer Journey

Over the coming week, try a whole new way of praying. Some morning or evening, when you can find a few minutes alone, try this. Stand as you pray, turn your hands upward, and look toward heaven. Then pray out loud. In your prayer, address God as Creator and thank him for all he has made, including you. Next, address him as Father and praise him for adopting you as his child through the sacrifice of Jesus on the cross. Ask for power to live faithfully as his loving child. Finally, address him as the Good Shepherd and pray for his leading in your life and for ears that hear and recognize his voice. Let this become one of the ways you pray with your eyes wide open.

Four

Power in Prayer

Prayer is the key that unlocks all the storehouses of God's infinite grace and power. All that God is, and all that God has, is at the disposal of prayer.

R. A. TORREY

Years ago I heard a Christian comedian, Ken Davis, talk about how Christians are like sheep. He designed a T-shirt with a picture of Jesus and a sheep. The picture is a lamb walking on its hind legs right in front of a ferocious lion and a menacing wolf. Both of the predators are glaring at the little lamb. Their eyes say one thing: "Lunch!" But walking next to the lamb is Jesus. As a matter of fact, Jesus is holding the lamb's little hoof as they saunter past the intimidating carnivores.

There is a text box over the lamb's head. The little, fluffy, vulnerable lamb says just a few words to the lion and the wolf. These words capture the theological and biblical truth that presence and power are linked together. The lamb says, "I'm with him," as he points to Jesus. There is the sense that the lamb will be safe because of who he is with. Presence and power are connected in the life of Christians because God's power becomes our power when we are near him and realize he is with us. When we pray with our eyes wide open, we see God's power unleashed over and over as we live in the presence of the omnipotent Son of God.

Presence and Power Are Intimately Connected

In the previous chapter we reflected on the presence and person of God. He is Creator, Father, and Shepherd. Each of these speaks of God's intimacy with us. When we walk in God's presence and are aware of this truth, prayers flow and heavenly power is unleashed. What we must learn is that the power we need is always God's, never ours. Powerful prayer is not about us leveraging, controlling, or convincing God of what he should do. It is not about speaking memorized scripts or clever incantations. It is about living in the presence of the one who holds all power in his heart and hands.

It is about humbly acknowledging our connection with our Creator, loving our Father, and following our Good Shepherd. Power is released when we focus more on who we are praying to than what we are praying about. The closer we live in fellowship with God and dwell in his presence, the more his power flows, because we come to know that his sovereignty is absolute, his will is immutable, and he is worthy of our absolute devotion. Living in God's presence and seeing his power unleashed through prayer are absolutely linked together.

I Am with You

Moses learned this truth when God called out to him from within a burning bush on Mount Horeb. God spoke to Moses and told him to return to Egypt and confront one of the most powerful leaders on the planet at the time, Pharaoh. Not only was Moses called to stand face-to-face with the mighty king, but he was instructed to ask if all of God's people could leave Egypt. Don't forget, these people were Pharaoh's slave labor on his massive construction projects. Moses's eyes were wide open to the challenge he faced. He could see that this would not go well from a human perspective. But his eyes were also open to see the greater reality of God's presence, power, and glory.

In this amazing encounter at the burning bush, Moses and God talked. This is a prayer encounter. Moses asked, "Who am I that I should go to Pharaoh and bring the Israelites out of Egypt?" (Exod. 3:11). God's answer seems strange at first glance. Instead of explaining who Moses was, God simply declared, "I will be with you" (v. 12). God assured Moses of his presence, thereby guaranteeing him the power he needed. The focus was not on Moses but on God. "Moses, all you really need to know is that I will be with you!" That was the message God communicated.

I have heard these words of Scripture ring loud in my heart and ears many times through my life as a follower of Jesus. When I go through a challenging time and find myself anxious and worried, as fear descends and darkness clouds the sky, I hear God speak, "I will be with you." When Kevin and I hit a bump in the marital road we travel together and I know the call is to die to self, I hear the voice of God, "I will be with you." A family member or friend is struggling to make sense of the trial they are experiencing. I wonder how I can help. Then God speaks, "Sherry, I will be with you and give you what you need to help that person." Just like Moses, I have a sense I can press forward. It is not about my strength, insights, or wisdom. It is about the God who is with me.

My prayer is that you will hear the voice of the God who shows up in burning bushes and times of desert wanderings.

He is with you. He really is. Just ask him. Focus on who he is, not who you are. We have limits; he does not. You might lack the power to make it through . . . you probably do. But when you pray with your eyes open to see his presence and hear the answer to your questions, he reassures you he is present. With God at your side, you are never alone. "If God is for us, who can be against us?" (Rom. 8:31). His power is always enough.

I AM

Moses was not done with his Q&A session with God. Next he asked about what he should say to the leaders of the people of Israel if they pushed back and did not believe that God had spoken to him: "Suppose I go to the Israelites and say to them, 'The God of your fathers has sent me to you,' and they ask me, 'What is his name?' Then what shall I tell them?" (Exod. 3:13). This is a fair question. In the ancient world, a name meant everything, and Moses knew the leaders would want an explanation of exactly who was calling them to rebel against Pharaoh. Who is this God that could overpower the mighty king of Egypt, and why should they trust Moses to lead them?

God's answer to this question was very similar to his answer to the first question. He said, "I AM WHO I AM" (Exod. 3:14). God declares, "I am the God who is." God is speaking of his being, his nature, and his presence. To further clarify, God goes on to tell Moses to explain that he is "the LORD, the God of your fathers—the God of Abraham, the God of Isaac and the God of Jacob" (Exod. 3:15). God explains that he is the one who is with us at all times. He had been with the patriarchs; he had led them for centuries. His presence and power would continue with his people. He is the eternal I AM.

When Moses felt inadequate and weak, he asked God, "Who am I?" and God's response was, "I am with you." When Moses asked, "What is your name?"—in essence, "Who are you?"—God responded by saying, "I Am." In both cases, God assured Moses of his presence, and this held the promise of power to make it through whatever he faced. God essentially answered both questions the same way: "I am with you."

Prayer Unleashes Heavenly Power

When we walk through each day with our eyes open to the presence of God, we will see his power unleashed. But to do this, we must pray. Could it be that we do not experience all the power God wants to give to us because we have not prayed? Dallas Willard spoke these words that transformed my understanding of prayer: "Learning to pray in the power of God is the primary place we learn to live with the power that God gives."[1] He taught me that seeking to live in the power of God without praying in power opens the door for pride and an inflated sense of our own abilities. It is too easy for us to begin giving ourselves credit for God's great works. Human hubris is staggering and power can be intoxicating. We must be ever aware that all the power that is unleashed in and through us is from God.

If we forget this reality, we can start thinking and acting, in subtle or overt ways, like we are the source of the work that God has accomplished. When we pray in power and trust in God, answers come. When they do, we are certain that only God could have accomplished the powerful deeds we see.

If we want to see heavenly power come into our lives, homes, churches, and world, we must pray for his power to work in and through us. When we do, God answers and gets the praise. When we pray in power, we learn that living in the power of

God should be normal. It is not an anomaly. As we give God the glory, he unleashes even more power.

As It Has Always Been

All through the history of the Bible, this has been the reality. Heavenly power is unleashed when the people of God open their eyes, see a need, and pray. The great Wesleyan Methodist preacher Samuel Chadwick wrote:

> There is no power like that of prevailing prayer—of Abraham pleading for Sodom, Jacob wrestling in the stillness of the night, Moses standing in the breach, Hannah intoxicated with sorrow, David heartbroken with remorse and grief, Jesus in sweat and blood. Add to this list from the records of the church your personal observation and experience, and always there is cost of passion unto blood. Such prayer prevails. It turns ordinary mortals into men of power. It brings power. It brings fire. It brings rain. It brings life. It brings God.[2]

Prayer brings God! I love that. And God always brings power, because he is unbounded power.

A cursory survey of the Bible shows this to be true from beginning to end. In the opening books of the Bible, we see that almost every significant character prays in power and sees answers to these prayers. The great patriarch Abraham cried out on behalf of king Abimelek and God responded with healing power (Gen. 20). Isaac prayed for God to open the womb of his wife Rebekah and she conceived twins (Gen. 25). Jacob prayed and wrestled with God and received a heavenly blessing (Gen. 32). Joseph prayed to God as a slave in a foreign land and God raised him up to the highest place in all the land, next to the king (Gen. 39–45). Judgment was falling on the people of Israel for their rebellion, and Moses prayed to God and the disaster ceased (Exod. 32). Joshua prayed and the sun stood still (Josh. 10). Gideon prayed and God prepared the way for victory (Judg. 6). Naomi prayed for God's blessing on Boaz and he received Ruth as his wife; they are both found in the genealogy of Jesus, the Savior of the world (Ruth 2 and 4; Matt. 1:5).

This continues through the rest of the Old Testament, as Hannah prayed and received a son, Samuel (1 Sam. 1–2). Then Samuel, the great prophet and judge of Israel, in his farewell speech prayed for the nation to be spared judgment for their hard hearts, and God answered his prayer (1 Sam. 12). Kings like David and Solomon prayed and saw heavenly glory released. Prophets like Elijah, Elisha, Jeremiah, and Isaiah prayed and God moved. Leaders like Nehemiah, Ezra, and Daniel cried out to God and saw heaven intersect with earth, and divine power was unleashed as walls were rebuilt, worship was restored, and deliverance was experienced.

The story of the New Testament continues the witness to the power of prayer. The church prayed for Peter while he was wrongly imprisoned, and God sent an angel to release him (Acts 12). The apostle Paul prayed for the early churches, and those churches helped plant other congregations that have passed down the legacy of the gospel to the bodies of believers we gather with today. Jesus prayed and the dead came to life (John 11). Scriptural stories of prayers being lifted up and answered in power could make up a whole book. As a matter of fact, they do—that book is called the Bible.

We not only see story after story of the power of prayer in the Bible, but we find direct teaching on this topic. In his letter to the Ephesian Christians, the apostle Paul writes this prayer:

> I pray that the eyes of your heart may be enlightened in order
> that you may know the hope to which he has called you, the

riches of his glorious inheritance in his holy people, and his incomparably great power for us who believe. That power is the same as the mighty strength he exerted when he raised Christ from the dead and seated him at his right hand in the heavenly realms. (Eph. 1:18–20)

The power the Father makes available to us in prayer as we walk with his Son is nothing less than the power that raised Jesus from the dead. This resurrection power is available to you and me. This is why Dallas Willard warns us that living in God's power must begin by praying in power.

God is ready to do things in and through you that will bring him glory and amaze you. The power God wants to release in our lives is too much for us to handle. But if we know it is his power, if it comes through bold and humble prayer, God will get the glory. In the chapters ahead, you will discover many ways to pray in power. As you learn to do this, you will see amazing results and be quick to give God all the praise, honor, and glory!

Your Prayer Journey

Over the coming week, pray before you walk into situations you know will be challenging, tough, or potentially conflict-oriented. Ask God to let you see his presence and power in the midst of these times. As you live through these situations, pray with your eyes open. Of course, pray silently but intentionally and consistently. In particular, address God as the great I AM who is with you at all times. Ask him to help you see his presence and sense his leading in these challenging times of your life.

PRAYING WITH **EARS**

WIDE
OPEN

LORD, hear my prayer, listen to my cry for mercy; in your faithfulness and righteousness come to my relief.... I spread out my hands to you; I thirst for you like a parched land. Answer me quickly, LORD; my spirit fails. Do not hide your face from me or I will be like those who go down to the pit. Let the morning bring me word of your unfailing love, for I have put my trust in you. Show me the way I should go, for to you I entrust my life.

PSALM 143:1, 6–8

The question is not, is God speaking? The issue before us is, are we listening? Do we hear the voice of the Creator of the universe? Are we attentive to the whispers of the Holy Spirit? Do we let God's Holy Word shape and transform our lives?

When we listen attentively and learn to recognize the voice of our Good Shepherd, we can enter holy conversations and engage with God in ways we had never dreamed were possible.

Five

God Is Speaking

Then you will call, and the LORD will answer;
you will cry for help, and he will say: Here am I.

ISAIAH 58:9

In the opening verses of the first chapter of the Bible, we read, "And God said . . ." (Gen. 1:3). With these words, the Lord of eternity began to speak all things into existence. In the last chapter of the Bible, God is still speaking. He says, "It is done. I am the Alpha and the Omega, the Beginning and the End. To the thirsty I will give water without cost from the spring of the water of life" (Rev. 21:6). At the consummation of all things, God is speaking. From beginning to end, the Scriptures reveal a God who speaks, engages, and communicates with his creation and guides the people he made and loves.

Through decades of walking with Jesus, I have learned this reality over and over again. God is speaking. Sometimes he whispers. At other times he shouts. At all times God is present and desiring to connect with you and me.

In the Beginning

God speaks in very personal ways. He does not give vague and obscure direction but crystal-clear leading for his people. The first man, Adam, learned this when his Maker spoke:

> The LORD God took the man and put him in the Garden of Eden to work it and take care of it. And the LORD God commanded the man, "You are free to eat from any tree in the garden; but you must not eat from the tree of the knowledge of good and evil, for when you eat from it you will certainly die." The LORD God said, "It is not good for the man to be alone. I will make a helper suitable for him." (Gen. 2:15–18)

When I read these words, I am struck by at least four things God spoke to Adam. Each one reveals something about God and also about us as his people.

I am the God who provides. Trees, trees, beautiful trees. Laden with fruit and pleasing to the eye and the taste buds. God tells Adam—and all of his children through the ages—that he provides because he loves us.

I am your protector. Beware of the poison that is in one particular tree. Don't eat it. It will kill you! God warns his first children and all those in the lineage of the human family. Sin destroys and God protects us with clear warnings.

I have a purpose for your life. The goodness of work was established before the fall. God gives his children meaning and purpose by giving them a garden to work and keep. In the same way, God loves us enough to give us meaningful labor and a reason to get out of bed each day.

I delight in your pleasure. Not only does God give sweet fruit, but he provides companionship and the pleasure of intimacy—a man and a woman together in a stunning garden. God commands them to be fruitful and multiply (Gen. 1:28; 2:25). God speaks pleasure to his beloved people.

As it was in the beginning, it is now, and so it will ever be. God speaks to his creation with boldness, clarity, and grace. The question is not, does God speak? The real issue is, are we willing to listen? (We will get into that topic in the next chapter.)

Years ago when Kevin and I served in youth ministry, there was a young student who came from a very difficult background. He placed his faith in Jesus, and we watched as his life was ignited with passion for God and a desire to live for Jesus. We got him a Bible and he devoured the Scriptures. For the first three or four weeks of his new life in Jesus, he was reading the Bible for over an hour each day. The words of the Bible were making sense, God was at work, and he was experiencing transformation.

One day he stopped reading. He shut the Bible and put it down. When we asked why he was no longer reading his Bible, he did not say, "Because it is hard to understand." He did not answer, "I don't really get anything out of it." This was his answer: "As I read the Bible, it tells me to stop doing things I like to do. It also points out things I should start doing that I am not sure I want to do. It is making me very uncomfortable." Wow, what profound honesty! He did not wonder if God still speaks. He struggled with how clearly the Holy Spirit communicated to his life through the Bible. On a happy note, after some prayer and a kind challenge, he got back to digging into the Word of God on a daily basis.

What Do We Mean When We Say "God Speaks"?

When some people hear statements like "The Lord told me" or "God said," they have red flags pop up and theological alarms go off in their mind. When we talk about God speaking, this language means very different things to various groups of people. Some faithful and passionate followers of Jesus believe God only speaks through the clear teaching of the Bible. In their theological framework, God stopped communicating in other ways once the Bible was completed and we had this revelation in our hands. Their understanding of the Latin term *Sola Scriptura* is that the Bible is not only the supreme authority for all matters of doctrine and practice, but it is also the only way God speaks today.

Other wonderful and committed Christians believe God still speaks in a variety of ways. Jim Samra, a pastor, teacher, and theologian, wrote a book that presents God speaking to his children in many and various ways. The title of the book says it all: *God Told Me: Who to Marry, Where to Work, Which Car to Buy . . . and I'm Pretty Sure I'm Not Crazy*. Not only is that a mouthful, but it is also a specific theological position that says God still speaks in many ways.

I believe the Bible is the final and absolute authority for all we believe and do. We measure everything by God's Word because it is absolutely true from beginning to end. If we ever have a sense that God is speaking to us, and what we hear is contrary to the teaching of the Bible, we are not hearing from God. The Holy Spirit will never speak, lead, or direct in a way that is contrary to the teaching of the Bible.

At the same time, I believe God speaks in a variety of ways that affirm and fit consistently with his Word. In the Old and New Testaments we see God speaking in many ways to his people, and

I see no biblical evidence that God now limits himself to only one form of communication. What we do is use the Bible as our measuring rod for all other times we believe God is speaking. Christians do not change our beliefs based on personal experience. Instead, we shape our lives to the clear teaching of the Bible.

God Is Speaking

I discovered this truth in fresh, new ways when I went through a challenging time related to a major surgery. I was training for a 25K run and my doctor told me I would have to skip the race because he needed to perform surgery on me around the same time as the race. I was disappointed because I loved to run and was near the end of my six months of training. The race was only a few weeks away and I would have to miss it.

My youngest son, Nate, could see my disappointment, so he made me an offer. He was only ten years old, but he brought me a strong challenge to do the race on my own the weekend before my surgery. He told me, "Mom, you can do the race and I will ride next to you on my bike." One of the event organizers got wind of my pre-race race and my upcoming surgery. She told the local paper my story. The next thing I knew, the *Grand Rapids Press* was interviewing my son and me and sharing my story to inspire other runners.

As I was preparing for my personal version of the "River Bank Run," I was also preparing for my surgery. I prayed a lot as I ran. I am not a big fan of surgery . . . but who is? I had been through other surgeries and always seemed to have a hard time coming out from under the anesthetic.

During the weeks prior to finding out about my need for surgery, a particular psalm was often on my heart. I believe the Holy Spirit kept putting Psalm 27, particularly the first verse, on my heart. I found myself reading it and meditating on the message as I ran. I love the whole psalm, but the first verse captured my heart: "The LORD is my light and my salvation—whom shall I fear? The LORD is the stronghold of my life—of whom shall I be afraid?" Through these powerful words of Scripture, God was breathing hope and confidence into my heart. I listened to the voice of God through his holy Word. God was speaking to me.

As I continued training, now for my pre-race experience, my eyes were open and I saw the glory of God's creation and the greatness of his majesty in the trees, the sky, and the landscape all around me. God revealed himself through the intricacies and expansiveness of his world. He was speaking and my confidence rose. It was springtime in Michigan, and as God was bringing the earth back to life after the harsh winter snows, it reminded me that he could certainly heal me and bring me back to full health after the surgery.

As I whispered my fears and frustrations to God about my upcoming surgery, I could hear the Holy Spirit of the living God whisper back, "I am with you. I have created you. I will never leave you or forsake you. You are my beloved daughter." Over and over, the simple truths I had learned from the time I was a little girl and all through my adult life came flooding into my heart and soul. God was speaking, reminding me of what I knew to be true.

In addition to all of this, God began to speak through my circumstances and situation. People who read the article in the paper shared words of encouragement with me. God used that article and my upcoming surgery to inspire people and also move them to pray for me, speak words of blessing, and cheer me on.

The night before my surgery, my subsided fears seemed to rear their ugly head. I remember praying to God, asking him to comfort me once again. God spoke in a fresh, sweet, and humorous way. My son Nate, the one who had encouraged me to run the race on my own, decided to motivate me in one more way. He knew I was still nervous about undergoing anesthesia and anticipating a rough recovery time. He knew one thing that worried me, among others, was that I might get up in the middle of the night and absentmindedly take a drink of water, which was forbidden before the surgery. So, with tender care, while I was sleeping, Nate was once again going to encourage me to finish a very different kind of race.

I woke up in the middle of the night, and as I got out of bed, I felt a piece of paper under my foot. Nate had placed it on the ground next to my bed, knowing I would find it there. As I began to read the note, I was staggered by God's goodness to speak to me through my son's encouragement once again. On the top of this sheet of paper he had written in large letters,

Psalm 27 Verse 1
    The LORD is my light and salvation—whom shall I fear? The LORD is the stronghold of my life—of whom shall I be afraid?

    Mom, Remember when you're out of surgery I will be praying for you. God will be with you. I love you, from Nate.

It was Psalm 27, the same Scripture I had felt the Holy Spirit prompting me to read and reflect on over the past days. I had never mentioned this to any of my boys, but I believe the Spirit of the Living God was speaking through my son. Right there, in his young handwriting, were the very same words God was speaking to me in a fresh way, reassuring me of his presence and power.

As I entered the bathroom, overwhelmed with God's goodness to me, there was a note taped to the faucet: "Don't drink!" My son had thought of everything. When I reached to lift the cover of the toilet seat, there was one more little note: "Don't even think about it!" I laughed. God was not only speaking to me through my son, he was also lightening my worry through my son's sense of humor.

Many Ways

I believe God speaks to us in many ways to guide us, comfort us, challenge us, and draw us near to his heart. This journey of preparing for my surgery revealed a number of ways he speaks.

God speaks through the Bible. On my journey, God used a particular psalm to comfort, strengthen, and bring me confident hope as I prepared for surgery. This should not surprise any follower of Jesus. The primary way God speaks, in all generations, is through the Bible. The apostle Paul wrote these words, inspired by the Holy Spirit: "All Scripture is God-breathed and is useful for teaching, rebuking, correcting and training in righteousness, so that the servant of God may be thoroughly equipped for every good work" (2 Tim. 3:16–17). If you want to hear God speaking to you and giving directions for every aspect of life, make a practice of opening the Word of God each and every day of your life.

The wisest Being in all the cosmos has given us his Word. Reading the Bible every day will connect us to God's voice. If you ever have a moment when you feel far from God and don't know where to go or what to do, immerse yourself in the beauty and truth of the Bible. When you open this glorious book and read it, you are hearing from God. If you are not a big reader, I would suggest you use a Bible app (BibleGateway or YouVersion are great options) and have your smartphone read the Bible to you. I know people who begin each day by listening to Scripture. It is transformational for them. In the ancient world, almost no one owned a Bible and many people could not read. But they heard the Bible read. Bible listening is not a cop-out—it is retro on a historical level.

*God declares his glory through **creation**.* As I trained for my race, ran, and prayed, the beauty and wonder of God's creation spoke to my soul and reminded me of his faithfulness. In Psalm 19 we read, "The heavens declare the glory of God; the skies proclaim the work of his hands" (v. 1). God's glory is revealed in oceans, mountains, deserts, butterflies, and even falling leaves.

When I was in college, I hit a time of desperation and depression. My first semester of college did not turn out to be the experience I had hoped for or anticipated. It was a major disappointment for me and left me disillusioned. A friend of mine, Maria, was a resident director (RD) at a neighboring college, so I sought her out for some counsel. I spoke of the events that contributed to this time of struggle and my doubts of God's direction and care. Maria reminded me that God does care about me, and that in the midst of what appeared to be a chaotic time, God cares about the big and little details of my life. She pointed to Scripture and assured me that God knows the number of hairs on our head, he knows when one sparrow falls, and he is the Creator of all. She then encouraged me to go outside and look at a leaf—one single leaf. She suggested I reflect on the detail and intricacy that God placed in one leaf. I did what she suggested. I went outside and picked up a leaf and looked at it carefully, and God spoke to me. Through the power of the Holy Spirit, this message went deep within my heart and mind and brought me hope at a time I was struggling to see hope for my future. As I looked at the leaf, God gently spoke to me and reminded me that if he spent time designing this one leaf in such a magnificent way, he could do the same with my life. It was at that moment hope was restored; I knew God was speaking personally to me. I found the reassurance I longed for and my spirit was lifted.

God guides and directs through his **Holy Spirit.** One reason I believe I made it through that time of struggle was that I sought God and asked him who I could go to for help. The Holy Spirit kept putting Maria's name on my heart. It made sense to me that God would direct me to her. I knew, as a resident director of a Christian college, she would be able to help me process this challenging time. I don't believe the idea to go to her came from me; it was the Spirit of God directing me to the right person he would use to help me through this difficult time.

God spoke to Elijah through the still small voice of his Spirit (1 Kings 19:12–13). Jesus assured us that his sheep recognize the voice of their Good Shepherd (John 10:4). There are details of life that the Bible does not address specifically, but God wants to direct our steps in these areas. The Bible is clear that God delights when a man and woman are joined in marriage together, but it does not tell us exactly who to marry. God cares about where we live, where we go to school, how we use our resources, and every other detail of our lives. We need the Spirit's leading in life's big and little decisions.

God leads, and sometimes stops us, through **circumstances.** If you read the book of Acts, paying special attention to how circumstances directed both Peter and Paul, you will find that open and closed doors became an indicator of God's leading. Sometimes a person would come and invite them to minister— an open door. At other times a town would become violent and drive them away—a closed door. Over and over the early church leaders let circumstances become one of the ways they would sense the Lord speaking and directing.

When Kevin and I moved from Michigan to central California, it was a challenging season. All of my family and many of my closest friends live in Michigan. By God's grace we were able to live and minister in Michigan for two decades and raise our boys near my family. But God called us to move and serve a church on the West Coast. As I struggled, I heard the Holy Spirit whisper in my heart to read Psalm 23, the great Shepherd's Psalm. The Holy Spirit of God impressed upon my heart that I should read this every morning as I got up. I had a sense that if I did not read this daily, I was not being obedient to God's whisper in my life at that moment. I didn't have a sense how many mornings that meant, I just knew I was to start a regular practice of reading this psalm. I read and prayed Psalm 23 daily for over two months. God comforted me and prepared me for a new chapter of life and ministry. He reminded me over and over that he would lead me to green pastures and heavenly peace.

When we arrived in California, we could not find a house we could afford or qualify to buy. Finally, after a lot of prayer, work, and a couple of months, a door opened and we got just the right home for this next chapter of life. After we had settled into our home, it struck me that there were lush green hills and pastures in the valley where we lived. I was chatting with a church member and was delightfully shocked when he said, "I don't know if you know this, but John Steinbeck, the famous American novelist, used this exact valley as the setting for one of his short stories." I asked which one. He replied, "The Pastures of Heaven." I had no doubt God was speaking and we were in the right home. We had arrived at our green pastures. I knew why God had spoken in a still small voice to read Psalm 23 every day. I had a sense that I had followed God's direction in reading this particular psalm every day, and now it all made sense. In that moment, God impressed on me that my daily practice of reading Psalm 23 could end.

God confirms his will and ways through people. All through the preparation for my race and surgery, God spoke to me through my son. God also used Maria to encourage me during a difficult time away at college. Both Nate and Maria loved Jesus and were responsive to the promptings of the Holy Spirit. All through the Bible, God uses people to speak. One of the most shocking examples is when God speaks through King Cyrus, a pagan leader (Ezra 1:1–4; 5:13–16; Isa. 44:28–45:1). If God could direct and speak to his people though a nonbeliever, how much more can he speak through those who love and follow him.

*God reveals himself through **dreams and visions**.* Many followers of Jesus, and even spiritual seekers, have visions and dreams that draw them closer to God. Dreams and visions are found all through the Bible. Abraham was comforted by a vision (Gen. 15:1). The apostle Paul had a vision that directed him to a time of ministry in Macedonia (Acts 16:9). God used both Joseph and Daniel to interpret dreams (Gen. 41:1–7 and Dan. 2:28). The Lord gave Solomon a dream to set the tone and direction of his kingship (1 Kings 3:5–15). God can and does reveal himself through visions and dreams.

A dear friend of our family, Nabeel Qureshi, grew up as a devout Muslim. After years of closely examining the Christian faith and his Muslim faith, he came to the conclusion that the Bible and the gospel are true. He also realized that what he had been raised to believe as a Muslim was not founded on historical fact. He was ready to receive Jesus as God and Savior.

His mind embraced the truth. But there was still a significant problem for Nabeel. His heart was holding back. His love for his family members, who were all Muslim, caused him to wait. In addition, all the years of hearing Muslim leaders declare that the Bible is untrustworthy, false, and corrupted caused lingering caution and doubts.

Nabeel came to a place where he believed in Jesus but still had some doubts in his heart. He prayed for God to give him a dream or vision about the truth of the Bible. He also prayed for courage to follow Jesus no matter what the cost might be.

God answered his prayer with a vision and three dreams. In these heavenly confirmations God assured Nabeel that the Bible is true and trustworthy. With these heavenly affirmations, Nabeel told his family and friends that he was leaving his Muslim faith and following Jesus. His story can be found in the book *Seeking Allah, Finding Jesus.* God graciously spoke and empowered Nabeel to move forward on his spiritual journey. And the vision and dreams lined right up with the teaching of the Bible.

The real question is not, does God speak? God is communicating all the time. The question most Christians and even non-Christians need to ask is, am I willing to listen and follow what God says? That is the question we must each answer.

Your Prayer Journey

Over the coming week, continue to grow in praying with your eyes wide open. Dare to invite another Christian, a family member, or a friend to pray with their eyes open. Share what you have been learning and experiencing and ask if they want to pray with you, with eyes open. Try to make this part of your time praying with others.

In addition, make a point of listening for God's voice and noticing various ways the Lord is speaking to you. Invite God to speak in any way he wants. As you read the Bible, pray, "Let me hear your voice as your Spirit leads me." When you go outside, ask God to let the heavens declare his glory and the earth to proclaim his creative beauty. Listen for the still small voice of the Spirit and be ready to respond. Take note of life circumstances that seem to have the fingerprints of God all over them. Be attentive to how God might be speaking through the people in your life. Prepare yourself in case God gives you a dream or vision that he wants to use to direct your life and speak to you. Be attentive all week long and take note of where God is speaking.

Six

Are You Listening?

Hearing God cannot be a reliable and intelligible fact of life except when we see his speaking as one aspect of his presence with us, of his life in us. Only our communion with God provides the appropriate context for communications between us and him.

DALLAS WILLARD

I believe there are sacred spaces all over this planet. The presence of the Holy Spirit saturates these places with a sweet holiness because the people of God have prayed deeply and consistently in these locations. It can be a living room where a family has read Scriptures, shared stories of faith, immersed themselves in intimate prayer, and shared deep joy that only comes through the presence of the Spirit of God. It can be the grounds of a Christian camp where children, young people, and families have worshiped with passionate voices, heard life-changing Bible messages, and met with Jesus, the Savior of the world. Church buildings, homes, even neighborhoods can become holy spaces as prayers are offered, worship is expressed, and the Word of God is read.

Kevin and I entered such a space in the spring of 2015. We were invited to do some ministry with leaders in the Chicago area. In particular, we were speaking to a group of leaders at the Billy Graham Center for Evangelism on the campus of Wheaton College. We stayed in a guesthouse on the college campus called the Harbor House. This space felt holy as we entered it. Many great and godly leaders had stayed in the humble and beautiful rooms of this house through the years. The guest book in our room gave testimony to this fact as we read the names of great and saintly men and women who had stayed there. You could almost feel the prayers lingering in the air and the presence of Jesus in this space.

Just across the street was the Wheaton College chapel. Kevin had attended worship services and student gatherings in this space over three decades earlier. The chapel had a bell tower just across from our bedroom window. It was three days into our time in the Harbor House when something happened that God used to teach me a profound lesson about prayer and listening to him.

It was nine in the morning and I was at the small wooden desk in the corner of the room. I was working on this book and thinking about prayer, God's love, and seeking to shape words that would help others grow in their passion and practice of prayer. All of a sudden the bell rang out with clear, beautiful, and loud tones. Nine distinct times the bell rang so clear that it seemed impossible to ignore.

Then it struck me, like a whisper from heaven. A simple idea. A profound truth. A sobering reality. Over the past three days there were many hours that I had not heard or noticed the bell ringing. It was there—loud, clear, undeniable. But I had missed it. In my busyness, in my distracted state, in my muddled mind, in the ordinary flow of the day, I had not noticed the ringing of the bell.

On day three on the campus of Wheaton College, it occurred to me that it was only when I was sitting quietly in my room, with my heart tuned in, that I noticed the chiming. When I silenced my mind and heart, my ears tuned in. I heard what had been there all along.

God whispered to my heart in that moment. I was reminded that he is consistently speaking to me. He is directing, inspiring, convicting, blessing, guiding, and talking . . . he really is. The problem is not that God fails to communicate with his children; the real issue is that we are distracted, busy, cluttered, loaded down with the cares of life.

Could our lives be like my experience in that cozy guesthouse on the college campus that cool spring morning? We live in sacred spaces; we exist and walk in the very presence of the God who is omnipresent and ever seeking to communicate with his children.

The bells are ringing. His voice is chiming. Are we quiet enough to hear and recognize the voice of the Lord who loves us and longs to connect with his beloved children?

If we are not careful, the ringing of the bells might even become an irritation. As we are consumed by life's demands and swept into the frenzied pace of our modern world, the chiming can be muted, and when it does cut through our distractions, we find ourselves annoyed. God's voice is there, but we take it as a disruption rather than a gift of grace.

It is time to pray with our ears wide open. God is speaking. He is seeking to communicate. The bells of his presence can be heard if we will listen. His whispers are consistent. If we will sit quietly and pay attention, we will hear from the lover of our soul. It is time to pray with our ears open in excited anticipation, realizing that the one who spoke in the beginning and created the heavens and the earth is still speaking. When we pray with our ears tuned in to the voice of God, a new journey of intimacy and prayer is right in front of us.

Make a Decision

As a church leader I have a lot of people ask me questions about prayer. One of the most common questions is, "How can I learn to hear from God?" I begin by telling them that God calls us his beloved children and the sheep of his pasture. Jesus assured us that he calls us by name, leads us, and we can recognize his voice (John 10:3–4). Hearing the voice of our Good Shepherd should be normative, not a rare exception. In these conversations I am emphatic that Jesus will always lead us in ways that are consistent with the Bible and never contrary to the clear teaching of Scripture.

Then I invite them to make a decision to listen for the voice of God. Through the years I have found that most people can develop a holy habit of hearing the voice of the Shepherd if they will be serious and intentional about this part of their spiritual life. Here is the process I have led many people through:

Sit, kneel, stand, lie down, or take a walk in a quiet setting. Find a posture that helps you seek God. Do all you can to remove distractions. In our world today, this could mean turning off devices that might ring, buzz, or cry out for our attention. For many people this is a painful, and in some cases an unthinkable, step in the process. You may want to have a journal or daily note card near to write down impressions, whispers, names, convictions of sin, words of encouragement . . . whatever you hear. I would encourage you *not* to write these notes down in your phone or tablet, because it might be preferable to keep those devices at a distance at this time. When you log on to a device, it can quickly drive your mind toward email, social media, or other possible distractions. However, if you are able to use your devices without being distracted, it is your choice to make. Wait quietly and jot down whatever comes to your heart. Wait on the Lord. Remain quiet. Keep your heart open. Train your ears and heart to be attentive.

Invite God to speak. This might sound strange since God is always ready to speak to us. But this invitation expresses your desire to hear his voice. Tell God that you long to hear him speak. Declare that you want to be ready to follow where he leads. Commit to do all you can, with his power leading you, to follow him.

Identify the source. Generally, when we hear something in this time of waiting on God, there are three potential sources: Sovereign God, self, or Satan. Ask yourself, "Is this coming from my own mind, thoughts, family history, worry, or from some place in my own heart and mind?" If it is, seek to set this aside. You can ask, "Do I have a sense that this is from the enemy? Is he seeking to confuse or mislead me?" The Scriptures are clear that the Evil One is the father of lies. In John 8:44, hear the description Jesus gives of the devil: "He was a murderer from the beginning, not holding to the truth, for there is no truth in him. When he lies, he speaks his native language, for he is a liar and the father of lies." If you have a sense that the Evil One is trying to mislead you, speak the name of Jesus and rebuke him. Remember that the Bible teaches, "Submit yourselves, then, to God. Resist the devil, and he will flee from you" (James 4:7). But if you have a conviction that what you are hearing is from the Lord, move to the next step.

Test it against Scripture. If the leading you are feeling lines up with the teaching of the Bible, continue to keep listening. If what you have heard is contrary to the teaching of the Bible, know that you are not hearing from God. The Holy Spirit of

God will never lead a child of God to act in a way that is against what is revealed in the Bible.

Take note of God's peace. As you act on the leading of the Spirit, you should experience some measure of God's peace. Jesus said, "I have told you these things, so that in me you may have peace. In this world you will have trouble. But take heart! I have overcome the world" (John 16:33). This doesn't always mean that just because you heard from the Lord, it will necessarily be easy, but I have found that there will be some measure of peace. God is Sovereign Lord over all things, and when he is present, his peace is nearby.

Get wisdom in community. God has made us for community, and asking for confirmation and wisdom from godly men and women can be very helpful. These should be people who walk closely with God and who you trust. Listen to their wisdom and invite them into a process of praying for and with you.

Submit and obey. Once you are confident you are hearing from the Lord, and it is in line with biblical teaching, submit to the leading of the Lord and obey his promptings. Sometimes this will be a call to repentance. At other times it will be a direction for an important life decision. It could be some direction toward serving, giving, or reaching out to someone. At this point your call is to humbly obey the Lord's leading. I believe as you respond in obedience to his promptings, it opens the door to hear his voice speaking to you more clearly. Disobedience distorts our capacity to hear clearly from God. Sin deafens us to God's voice.

Learn to recognize the voice of the Good Shepherd. As you grow confident that you heard from the Lord and acted faithfully, remember how you heard from him. As time passes, you will discover that you are hearing his voice with increasing clarity and confidence. You will grow in your sensitivity to hear his voice throughout the activities of your day.

Asking Good Questions

Years ago my husband told me that he sometimes waits on the Lord in prayer and asks God specific questions. I had never really done this, but ever since Kevin encouraged me to try it, this has become part of my spiritual journey of listening for God's voice. I have discovered that specific questions will often yield very specific answers.

Some of the questions I have learned to ask God bring answers that lead to encouragement and blessing. Other questions, which are not as easy to ask, can lead to conviction and a call to repentance. I love to hear from the Lord, even when the word is one that stretches me and calls me to humble confession and repentance.

Here are some of the questions Kevin shared with me that he asks God. I would encourage you to do the same, and as you do, wait quietly and humbly for an answer.

- How much do you love me?
- In what ways are you showing me your love that I have not been paying attention to or noticing?
- In what areas of my Christian journey do you see me growing and becoming more like Jesus? How would you have me stay on this growth trajectory and go even deeper?
- Who is a person in my life that you want me to serve and show your love to in some tangible way? What would you have me do?
- Who is a person you have placed in my life that is not yet your follower but you want me to walk with them toward Jesus? What is our next step in this journey together?
- What is a hidden attitude or motive in my heart that does not honor you? How would you have me repent and change in this specific area?

- What is a pattern of continuing sin and disobedience in my life that I have become so comfortable with that it no longer bothers me? How do you feel about this sin, and what change needs to happen in my life to honor you?
- Who is one person in my family, church family, or neighborhood that needs a word of encouragement?

I encourage you to take time on a weekly basis to sit quietly and ask God specific questions like these, anticipating definitive answers. Since the Bible is our ultimate authority and the standard by which we judge all things, we must be people who are immersed in the Scriptures. If you are not opening the Bible on a regular basis and learning from the clear and unchanging revelation of God, I would suggest you begin there. Once this is a firm part of your spiritual growth, add a discipline of listening for the voice of the Spirit, ask great questions, and test what you hear against the truth of the Bible.

Voice Recognition

There are certain people whose voice you recognize with absolute confidence. You could hear their voice from a distance, you could have your back turned to them, you could hear only a few words, but you would know their voice. No doubt.

God desires that his children recognize his voice with this level of clarity. The Good Shepherd of your soul is ready to speak in such a way that you know when it is his voice. In the ancient world, shepherds would gather their sheep into a safe enclosure at night. Often, when there were two or more shepherds, their sheep would all share the same space. How in the world would the shepherds separate the sheep when the sun rose, the earth woke up, and it was time for them to take their sheep out of the pen?

The answer is simple. Each shepherd would stand by the gate of the sheep pen and call his sheep. A shepherd could speak, play a song on a flute, or even sing, and all of their sheep would pop their heads up, look at the shepherd, stand, and start filing out of the enclosure. This is still the case in places of the world where multiple shepherds graze their flocks in the same area. The sheep know the voice, the song of their shepherd. In the same way, when God calls or sings to you and me, our heads should pop up and we should look for Jesus. Then . . . we follow.

I don't want to make this sound too simple, but I also do not believe it needs to be overly complex. It is a journey of learning to listen and recognize the voice of our Lord, the Good Shepherd.

In my journey I have had many moments when the voice of God grew stronger and I learned to recognize it with growing clarity. One such time happened when I was a young schoolteacher in California. I loved teaching second grade and had every intention of signing my contract for another year at Ontario Christian Elementary School. The day I planned to sign my contract, something strange happened. I got a tickle in my throat. It would not go away. Water, coughing, and throat lozenges did not help. So I asked the principal if there was any way he could get a sub for my class. I had never done this before.

A short time later I was in my VW driving on the freeway and heading home. I was amazed at how quickly they had found a sub but delighted that I would not have to struggle through the whole day teaching and coughing incessantly. Then, like a switch being turned off, the tickle went away and the coughing stopped. I was already on the way home and they had a substitute, so I kept driving, thinking the tickle would certainly come back, but it did not.

I have always been a rule follower, so when I got home, I went to bed. I thought this was the proper thing to do. As I lay there, I did not feel sick. I was not tired. But something else happened. In the next few hours God began speaking to me. And the whole trajectory of my life changed!

The only way I can describe it is that I began to wrestle with God in prayer. Like Jacob, I spoke with God and he spoke to me. We wrestled and he won . . . he always does!

My plan was to keep teaching as Kevin went through seminary and finished his master of divinity. I had thought about getting a master's in education after Kevin was ordained and had a job as a pastor, but at this point in our lives, I was our primary source of income. Kevin worked full time at a church, but the pay was very modest and we could not make it without my income.

As I lay in bed, pondering how well I felt and wondering why the tickle had come so fiercely and gone away so quickly, the God of heaven spoke. I heard with my spiritual ears, not my physical ears. But the message was crystal clear and I recognized God's voice: "Don't sign your teaching contract. Go to seminary with Kevin."

In this moment, as in many moments in my life, I knew God was speaking because I responded and entered the conversation. "Lord, I am the family income, I can't stop teaching. We will have no money to pay our rent and bills." The message from the Lord remained. I heard it clearly. We wrestled on. I explained to God that I had taken one theology class in my undergraduate work, and it stretched and challenged me more than any class. When that class was done, I had breathed a sigh of relief and said, "I will never have to take another theology class again!" Of course God knew all of this, but I told him anyway. We wrestled on.

I felt a growing conviction that I must stop teaching and get a degree in theology. It did not make sense. But I recognized the voice of my Good Shepherd and continued to talk with him about my "concerns." Eventually God took a more firm tone. He asked me, "Do you want to be in my will?" I humbly responded, "Yes, Lord, I want to be in your will." He affirmed what I had heard earlier, "Then go to seminary." A measure of peace came over me. I knew what I had to do. I was unsure of how we would make it and what people would think of my decision, but it had become clear that God was speaking to me. I knew I would not sign my contract.

At this point, I began to contact a few trusted people and share what I believed God was speaking into my life. As I got counsel from other wise Christians (including my parents) over the next couple of hours, I received affirmation. Even my principal, who really appreciated having me on his teaching staff, said that it did not surprise him at all, and he believed it was the right thing for me to do.

Before the day was over, I had met with an administrator at the same seminary Kevin was attending and discovered that they had a "Team Ministry Grant" that covered 75 percent of the tuition of a second person of a married couple attending Fuller Theological Seminary together. I would pursue a master's in their School of Theology with an emphasis on Christian Formation and Discipleship the coming term. From this point on, I had many moments to trust that the God who called me would be the God who would provide.

As I look back on those years, I remember how much they stretched me. I also recall those years with great fondness. I am thankful I heard the Shepherd's call and followed.

Hindrances to Hearing God

God is speaking. The real issue is, are we listening? If God is speaking with clarity, then why don't we hear him more often? Why don't we respond with greater confidence? In the same way that there are conditions that help us hear God's whispers and words with greater clarity, there are also things that get in the way of us hearing from God. These need to be identified and overcome if we want to walk through our days praying with our eyes and ears wide open.

Unbelief—Prayer is not a magic incantation designed to get what we want from God. It is a conversation, a relationship, an encounter with God. If we do not believe in God and if we have not met his Son Jesus Christ, we have not entered this relationship. If we don't trust God to speak and we refuse to believe that he still is interacting with his children, it is very unlikely that we will hear his voice, even when he shouts.

We counter this obstacle by entering a personal relationship with God through faith in Jesus. When we trust that the Good Shepherd still speaks and his sheep can and should recognize his voice, we find that we can listen to and hear from him.

Mental Clutter—Have you ever looked for an article of clothing in a closet that is packed so full of random stuff that it is hard to close the door? Sometimes our minds and hearts can be cluttered with worry, fear, and even bad theology. This makes it hard to hear when the Holy Spirit is whispering or speaking.

If we want to hear God with greater clarity we need to un-clutter our minds by filling them with Scripture. This will help drive worry and fear away. The truth of God's Word helps us order our lives and thinking around the things that honor him.

Busyness—The faster we move, the harder it is to hear. Imagine a person trying to talk with you while they are standing and speaking at a normal volume. If you are in a car driving 70 mph by a person standing on the sidewalk trying to talk with you at a normal volume, it is unlikely that you will hear anything they say as you go screaming by. If you are riding a bike, you will pick up a few words—maybe even a whole sentence. If you are walking by, you will hear quite a bit more. But if you stop, face the person, and give your full attention, you will hear with much greater clarity. Our pace impacts how we hear anyone who is speaking to us. This is true as we seek to listen to and hear a spouse, a child, a friend, and even God. There is something about the sheer speed of a busy heart and life that makes listening prayer difficult.

As we learn to slow down, to be quiet, and to listen, we hear God more often and with greater clarity. This means adjusting the pace of our daily schedule and the flow of our week. I am convinced that one of the reasons God calls his children to slow down one day a week and enjoy the gift of a Sabbath is that he knows we need to hear from him and our busy lives can get in the way. As fewer and fewer Christians have a rhythm of weekly Sabbath rest, fewer people seem to hear from God. I encourage you to make a point of setting up a time of quiet in the flow of each day to meet with God and listen to him. In addition, you would be wise to develop a pattern of Sabbath each week where you dial back your pace and find a place of rest in God.

Negative View of Self—"Why would God speak to me?" "I am not good enough to hear from God." Many people today have decided that God would not speak to them directly. "God might speak to a pastor, priest, or church leader, but not someone like me." If we think this way, we will likely miss the wonderful things God is saying.

The antidote to this sickness of mind is the truth we have already discussed. We are God's precious creation, we are the sheep of his pasture, and we are his beloved children. When we see ourselves through the eyes of God, we realize that he wants to speak to us, his sons and daughters.

Untrained Ears—Many people have simply never learned to hear and recognize the voice of the Good Shepherd. Their ears are untrained. By using the simple process discussed in this chapter and developing your hearing, you can learn to recognize the voice of your heavenly Father.

A Sinful Lifestyle—When we are living in open rebellion to God and brazen disobedience to his Word, our ears can become deaf to his voice. It is not that God stops speaking; it is that we are simply unable to hear. When the Holy Spirit has convicted us over and over and we have persistently ignored his promptings, we learn to block out God's heavenly voice. When we are perfectly aware that we are living in opposition to the will of God and we don't care, it becomes hard to hear new and fresh words from God.

Confession and repentance are the only way to overcome the hindrance of a sinful lifestyle. We must identify our sin and tell God we are deeply sorry. We also need to repent and change our behavior, attitude, and choices. Being sorry is not enough. We need to be changed! When we turn from our sin and follow the teaching of Scripture and the conviction of the Holy Spirit, our ears are open and tuned in to hear from our Lord.

———

God is speaking. More than we imagine or dream, God is seeking to connect with us each and every day. We need to listen. We must take seriously the need to hear from God and remove the hindrances that stand in the way. When we recognize God's voice, we discover that he is not only speaking but also listening for us to engage with him. When this happens, we are ready to enter into two-way conversation with the Maker and Ruler of the universe, and this is exciting beyond measure.

Your Prayer Journey

Over the coming week, try three exercises that will tune your ears in to the God who is speaking to you: First, make a decision that you want to hear God with greater clarity. Use the process in this chapter that begins with coming before God quietly in a posture that fits what is happening in your heart. Move through the process and see if it helps you tune your heart to the heart of God and open your ears to whatever way he wants to speak to you. Second, take time to ask God specific questions, and wait quietly and expectantly for answers. You might want to have something to write with so you can collect thoughts God places on your heart and speaks to you. You can use the questions from this chapter or come up with your own. The key is patience as you listen. And always weigh what you hear against the teaching of the Bible. Finally, take time to pray through the hindrances listed in this chapter. Are any of these getting in the way of you hearing from the Lord? If the Holy Spirit convicts you that there is something standing between you and the Lord who loves you, deal with this hindrance with humility and tenacity.

Seven

God Is Listening,
Are You Speaking?

One great reason for prayerlessness is the lack of the living, joyous assurance that God will hear us. But if God's servant gets a vision of the living God waiting to grant their request, and to bestow all the heavenly gifts of the Spirit they are in need of, for themselves or those they are serving, how everything would be set aside to make time and room for this wonderful power that ensures heavenly blessing—the power of faith!

ANDREW MURRAY

Contrary to popular opinion, prayer is not primarily about getting what we want from God. It is about entering into God's plan for us. Prayer is not about getting ahold of God, it is about the Lord of the universe getting ahold of us. I learned this lesson in a powerful way while sitting on the sidelines of a soccer game. While cheering on my son, God captured my heart and taught me how to speak to him in personal and powerful ways that are consistent with his will.

There I sat, with all the soccer moms and dads on the sidelines. It was a sunny Michigan day and I was ready to fully engage in this experience, and even to pray!

I prayed with eyes wide open, intently watching my son and his teammates as they warmed up for the game. "Lord, help my son's team to win. They have practiced so hard and a win would be such an encouragement to them, in the name of Jesus, Amen."

As I was praying, my eyes fell on the line of soccer moms and dads on the other side of the field. These were the parents of the kids on the opposing team. Their children were wearing different-colored jerseys than our kids, and they were warming up on the other side of the field. As I continued to pray for our team while looking a little closer at those parents, I recognized a number of them because they attended our church.

Right in the middle of my prayer for our team to be victorious, it hit me—these other parents were probably praying the same thing. They wanted their children to have a great day, score some goals, and experience the affirmation of winning. It struck me that we parents, on opposite sides of the field, might just be putting God in a bit of a conundrum. What is the Lord of glory to do when parents from the same church, who all love their children and all believe in the power of prayer, are praying in direct opposition to each other?

Up to this point in my day, my prayers had been a monologue. I was letting God know what I would like. When this dilemma hit me, however, I shifted to a prayer that was a dialogue. Instead of just telling God to grant our team victory, I asked God, what should I pray? I wondered what Jesus would pray if he were in such a situation.

I thought of Jesus' teaching in the Gospel of John when he said, "And I will do whatever you ask in my name, so that the Father may be glorified in the Son. You may ask me for anything in my name, and I will do it" (John 14:13–14). Does this verse promise that I get whatever I want as long as I ask in prayer and give a hearty "In the name of Jesus" at the end of my supplication? What if two Christians are asking for opposing things? Does God become the great heavenly tiebreaker? Is there more to prayer than me simply getting what I ask?

The kids were still stretching and the game had not even started and my head was already spinning with this theological quandary. "Lord, is it wrong to pray for my son's team to win?" I had a deep conviction in my heart that it was not wrong, in a sinful way, to pray this, but that there were better ways to pray. I asked the Lord, "Teach me to pray. Show me how to communicate with you in situations like this. I want to be a person of prayer, but I suspect that sometimes my prayers are too narrow and self-serving."

The Holy Spirit responded by flooding my mind and heart with new ways to pray. Rather than simply asking for victory for half the kids on the field, why not pray for each child to play to the best of their ability? Why not pray for each player to have fun and stay safe and injury free? This would allow me to pray for each child, no matter what color jersey they were wearing. I began to pray, moving my eyes from child to child. By now the game had started, so I prayed for these athletes as they ran, kicked, dove, and sometimes fell down. I felt the Lord prompt me to pray for each child who knew Jesus to grow in Christlikeness, whether they won or lost. I prayed for each Christian parent, including myself, to behave well, no matter if our child won or lost.

By the time the game was over, I had learned to talk to the God who listens. And I discovered more about listening to the

God who speaks. It is interesting to me as I write this story, I can't remember if my son's team won that game, but I will never forget what I learned about speaking to the God who is always listening. So no matter how the game turned out, the day brought a big win because all the kids received the blessings of prayer.

God really is listening. He wants us to speak to him. He loves when his children communicate with their heavenly Father. The problem is that our prayers are often too small. We ask for victories at sporting events, we request toys that break and rust, and we cry out for transitory pleasures.

When Jesus said, "And I will do whatever you ask in my name, so that the Father may be glorified in the Son. You may ask me for anything in my name, and I will do it" (John 14:13–14), we often rush to the "ask me for anything" and miss the heart of Jesus' words. What if Jesus is trying to teach us how to speak intimately and effectively with God? What if this passage is not primarily about us getting requests we really, really want? What is Jesus getting at in this often-quoted and rarely understood passage?

Three Lessons about Speaking to God

It is important that we understand the context of Jesus' words in John 14. Although there are still seven more chapters in the Gospel, we are actually drawing near the close of Jesus' life and ministry. The cross is looming and the end is near. Jesus taught in the upper room, he instituted the sacrament of communion, and he washed the disciples' feet. Shortly after this he lifted up his High Priestly Prayer and gave his final detailed instructions to his followers before going to the cross to pay for our sins.

When Jesus teaches about prayer in John 14:12–14, we should tune in and prepare to learn. His words are bold and epic. The promises seem almost too big to believe. Jesus says things such as, we will do the kind of works he has been doing, we will do greater things than what he had done, and we could ask for anything in his name and he would do it. This sounds like a blank check and an absolute promise. But when we look closer, we learn that God is inviting us to speak, listen, and trust his wisdom. What is Jesus teaching us about speaking to the God who is always listening?

God invites us to ask. Since God is listening, he is ever ready to hear our prayers and receive our requests. But God is not a Santa Claus who waits for our list of the presents we want once a year. He is not a heavenly Buddha whose belly we rub for good luck to get what we want. He is not our lucky rabbit's foot that we keep in our pocket and take out when we need a little heavenly magic. James is painfully clear when he writes, "When you ask, you do not receive, because you ask with wrong motives, that you may spend what you get on your pleasures" (4:3). God wants us to ask, but he is not raising spoiled children who demand whatever they want and pout if they don't get their requests in the right size, style, or at the requested time.

We are to ask with humility and wisdom. God wants to hear our desires and passions, but he delights when these are being shaped and formed by his presence in our lives and his will for the world around us.

*We are to do this **in the name of Jesus**.* After assuring us that God wants us to ask of him, we are instructed to pray in the name of Jesus. For so many of us, this means that we tag the words "In the name of Jesus" on the end of our prayer. If we are not careful, we can treat these words like a magic incantation we believe assures us we will get what we want from God. Is that what Jesus is seeking to teach his people right before he goes to the cross and dies in our place for our sins?

There is much more going on here than meets the eye. When Jesus calls us to pray in his name, he is calling us to pray as he would pray. When an ambassador represents a country and speaks in its name, this person stands as a representative and they are to speak only what is consistent with the will of the sovereign state they represent. Ambassadors do not say whatever they want and place the weight of a country behind their words. Instead, they are to faithfully represent the name and will of their country. In the same way, when we pray in the name of Jesus, we are declaring that our prayer is consistent with the heart of Jesus and the will of the Father.

Our requests and the fruit of our prayers are meant **to bring glory to the Father.** When we ask with humility and wisdom, and when we pray consistently with the heart of our Savior, the third part of Jesus' teaching follows naturally. Our prayers will bring glory to the Father. When we pray, we should always be asking the question, would this bring praise and honor to the God who saved me? Will this prayer, if answered in the affirmative, lift up God and glorify his holy name?

Lord, Teach Us to Pray

One day Jesus was with his followers and he was praying. One of his disciples made a beautiful and wise request: "Lord, teach us to pray" (Luke 11:1). In this setting, and in Luke's Gospel, Jesus gives them a simple version of a prayer he taught many times and in many settings:

> Father,
> hallowed be your name,
> your kingdom come.
> Give us each day our daily bread.

Forgive us our sins,
    for we also forgive everyone who sins against us.
And lead us not into temptation. (Luke 11:2–4)

Look at this brief but potent prayer. It reinforces the same three things Jesus taught in John 14. Line by line we see the invitation to ask. But the asking is wise and it is not about petty and self-centered things. Each line reflects the heart of Jesus and is in line with his will. And each request, if it were answered in the affirmative, would give glory to the God of heaven.

Speaking to the God Who Is Listening

My aunt Zelma was a wonderful woman of God who had influenced my faith through my childhood and into my adult years. She had outlived her husband and two of her three sons. Her faith seemed to get stronger with each passing year and every tragedy she weathered.

One day my phone rang and my mother explained that Aunt Zelma was drawing near the end of her life and she would be moving into a hospice center a few miles from my home. This meant she would be farther from my mom but quite close to me. I had a clear sense in my heart that God was giving me the honor of caring for a dear family member who had served so many others through her life.

When I got off the phone, I whispered a prayer with eyes wide open: "God, I am available, I would love to minister to my aunt in her last days." In these moments I sometimes raise a hand, like a little girl in a school class, as if to say, "Teacher, choose me!" I let God know I am up for whatever he wants to bring my way.

Soon after this I went to the hospice center to see Aunt Zelma, but the caregivers were fully engaged with her. It was clearly a bad time, so I slipped out without being noticed and decided to come back another time soon. The second time I went by, she was not in her room, so again I left and committed to try again soon. The third time was not the charm. When I came to her room, her pastor was with her, working on the details of her funeral. It was clearly inappropriate for me to barge in on their time together. Strike three.

As I walked out of the hospice center, I began to pray: "God, I can't believe how bad my timing has been. I do really want to be present for Aunt Zelma. Could you please help me? You know my heart, Lord, I don't want her to be alone in these last days." I didn't think much about my prayer, because short little prayers as I walk with my eyes open are a normal part of my life.

A few days later, at about 4:30 in the afternoon, I was picking some clothes up from the dry cleaners. As I was standing in line, I felt the Holy Spirit nudge me to go visit my aunt. I remember dismissing the thought because I really needed to get home to start dinner. The stirring continued, and the Lord brought to my memory the prayer I had lifted to God just a few days before. Could this be God's Spirit answering my request to be used by him in these last days of Zelma's life?

I called Kevin as I left the dry cleaners and shared what was happening. He encouraged me to go visit her. As I walked in and introduced myself to the woman at the front desk, she quickly let me know that the timing of my arrival was perfect. My aunt's only living son had been there earlier, but he had left a short time before, and she had just taken a significant turn for the worse. Zelma was drawing near the end. They had been trying to reach the son, but to no avail.

When I entered her room, I found my precious aunt with a sweet hospice nurse by her side. I took the seat on the other side of the bed. She was coherent but struggling a bit. My aunt Zelma breathed a sigh of relief to have me by her side. I assured her I would not leave. I sat quietly. I read some psalms with her permission. I softly sang a few hymns. It was obvious her time to leave and be with Jesus was drawing near.

As we entered the third hour of being together, I prayed a simple prayer in my heart asking God to direct me as I sought to think of more passages that would be appropriate. I waited quietly and felt a clear prompting to read Psalm 27, knowing how much that passage has ministered to me. I began reading,

> The LORD is my light and my salvation—
> whom shall I fear?
> The LORD is the stronghold of my life—
> of whom shall I be afraid? (vv. 1–2)

As I finished the second verse, I glanced up and looked into her eyes. I could sense God's presence in the room. It was palpable. I reassured her that the Lord was with her. It was in that moment she slipped away into the arms of her Savior. The Good Shepherd came, took his precious lamb on his shoulders, and brought her to green pastures.

As I walked out of the hospice center that night, I couldn't help but reflect on God's graciousness to hear my prayer. The God who listens knew my heartfelt longing that Zelma would be with loved ones at the end of her life. The God who speaks alerted me to the exact time she needed me to be there. On the other three occasions, my timing was not right. I responded to God's prompting and his timing was perfect.

While sitting at her funeral a few days later, her pastor stood up and began to share that it was hard to pick just a couple of passages for the service because Zelma had so many favorites. Then he said, "I do know one passage that was particularly meaningful for Zelma. It was Psalm 27." He opened his Bible and began to read:

> The LORD is my light and my salvation—
> whom shall I fear?
> The LORD is the stronghold of my life—
> of whom shall I be afraid?

These were the words that Zelma heard as she slipped from this life and entered her heavenly home.

Praying throughout our day with our eyes open will lead to experiences that honor God and bless those around us. Talking to God in two-way communication leads to moments when we see God responding to our heart's cry to be a servant who honors him. Speaking to the God who listens and listening to the God who speaks makes every day an adventure. It leads to sacred moments where God shows up and heaven intersects with earth in tangible and beautiful ways.

Your Prayer Journey

Each time you pray in the coming week, begin by saying, "Lord, I want my prayer to be in the name of Jesus. Please let all I pray be motivated by Jesus, consistent with the heart of Jesus, and for the glory of Jesus." If you are not confident your prayer reflects the will and desire of Jesus, slow down and ask yourself if you should be praying in this manner. If you are confident your prayer is consistent with the desires of the Savior and honoring to your heavenly Father, when you finish your prayer, speak these words with authority and confidence: "In the name of Jesus, Amen!"

Eight

Holy Conversations

To be with God, there is no need to be continually in church. We may make an oratory of our heart wherein to retire from time to time to converse with Him in meekness, humility and love. There is not in the world a kind of life more sweet and delightful than that of a continual conversation with God.

BROTHER LAWRENCE

It was our one-year anniversary, and Kevin's parents had kindly given us a dinner out and a night away at a local hotel. We were beyond broke, so this was a really big deal for us. At that time in our married life we did not eat out at nice restaurants—too expensive. We did not go to hotels—no reason for it. So this was a special time. I should have been happy and content. Instead, I found myself frustrated with my husband.

What bothered me was something that I had been noticing for over a year now. I had not articulated my frustration to Kevin, but things came to the surface on that morning in our hotel room. We had both taken time reading our Bibles and praying. As we had done so many times before, we talked about what we learned from the Scriptures. While sharing, Kevin mentioned that while he was praying, the Holy Spirit had spoken to him and put a number of things on his heart.

That is when I started feeling agitated. Kevin would often talk about prayer as if it were a conversation with God. He acted like he heard from God as he would hear from a friend. Honestly, it bugged me. I had never said anything, but this day it just came out.

"Kevin, you share with me often things God speaks to you. I know we can talk to God, and I am confident he hears us. But I don't hear God speaking to me, at least not like you describe it."

Kevin went on to explain that his prayers often included speaking and listening. Holy conversations. Familiar but sacred at the same time. He told me that he recognized God's voice like he recognized the voices of his parents and friends and my voice.

Honestly, this did not help my frustration. I said, "I have been a Christian since I was five years old. I believe the Bible. I love Jesus. I pray a lot, but I don't hear God speaking to me in a voice I recognize."

My husband, who was not known for his sensitivity in our early years of marriage (and he would agree with me on this), looked at me and said words that hurt and challenged me at the same time: "If you don't hear God speaking to you and if you don't recognize his voice, I believe that is your fault."

I looked at him and was not sure how to respond. Finally I said, "What do you mean?" He went on to ask me, "Do you expect to hear from God? Do you ask questions of God and wait for answers? Have you sought to recognize his voice? Do you believe that God still speaks to his children?"

These questions launched me on a spiritual quest. In that moment, the truth of God's Scriptures cascaded over my heart that God loves all his children, and if he would speak to Kevin, wouldn't he also speak to me? What good parent speaks to one child but not another? Maybe God was speaking, but I was just not noticing and responding.

I was moved to deeper places of prayer than I had ever imagined or experienced before. I began waiting quietly on the Holy Spirit. I started asking God questions and expecting my heavenly Father to answer. And over the next year my spiritual life was transformed. I found myself engaged in holy conversations where I would speak to God and listen for his voice. Within a couple of years I found myself conversing with God, eyes wide open, at many times and in many places during my day. I even had a prayer chair at our home in Michigan, and at times I would hear the Holy Spirit whisper, "Go to your prayer chair, be still, I want to speak with you." This became a normative and common part of my walk with Jesus.

The "Where" of Holy Conversations

The beauty of praying with your eyes wide open is that you can converse with God anywhere and anytime. Although I have a chair where I love to sit and talk with Jesus, the vast majority of my prayer time is not in the quiet of the morning when I sit in my chair. My holy conversations happen in stores, restaurants, while driving, on hikes, and even in places that don't seem "holy" at first glance. Ordinary and secular places become sacred when we engage in holy conversations.

I have a friend who is a medical doctor. He prays before every surgery and procedure he does. If the patient makes the request, he will pray with them in the operating room in the presence of the anesthesiologist and nursing staff. In these situations the prayer is lifted out loud. At other times, his dialogue with God is done quietly in his heart. He is speaking and listening as he does his work.

By the way, this doctor works in a very secular setting, not a Christian hospital. But he would tell you that he can't do his job to the best of his ability without speaking to God and listening for the wisdom and leading of the Holy Spirit.

I've Got This!

I knew Rod for two and a half decades. He grew up going to church. His Christian faith was genuine. He read his Bible, prayed, and tried to let his relationship with Jesus impact his life. Those who knew him well also knew he had times when he struggled with intimacy with God. When Rod became part of our family, I liked him immediately. He was a gentle and unassuming man with a warm smile and a kind disposition. He was also a wonderful father to my niece and nephew.

When we received word that he had cancer, it was a blow to our whole family. When the cancer advanced to the point where only a miracle would save him, we were all concerned for Rod. We were also praying for Kristin and Matt because we knew the loss of their dad would be very painful.

In November Rod contacted me because he heard that Kevin and I would be in Michigan a short time before he was to have a complex brain surgery. He wanted to meet with some family members and most importantly with the kids. True to his character over all the years we knew him, he was not concerned about himself. He was mostly concerned for Kristin and Matt as there was a high probability that they would be moving into the adult years of their life without him. He was selfless, all the way to the end.

During the family gathering, Rod shared what I would call his "burning bush" moment. He had entered into a holy conversation and he did not even see it coming. Rod had a clear sense that his life may be drawing to a close. The doctors were clear that the cancer was widespread and advanced. On the day this reality hit him hard, he was driving in his truck, and God showed up. Rod's eyes were open and so were his ears. Just like Moses heard God speak words of comfort and hope, so did Rod. "I was driving my truck down the road and getting ready to turn on 112th Street. I was feeling the weight of not being there for Kristin and Matt. Then it happened. I heard God speak. With absolute clarity I heard the words, '*I've got this!*'"

He went on to explain that he had heard people talk about God speaking to them, but he never really understood what they meant. He never fully believed what they were claiming. Rod looked at us and said, "Now I know it's true. I know people hear from God. I have experienced the presence of God." From that day onward we all saw a noticeable difference in Rod's walk with Jesus. We could all see on his face and hear in his voice that this was a real encounter with the living God.

For most of his life, he had spoken to God in prayer. Now he heard God speak to him. He was overjoyed. Rod's life changed, his faith grew deeper, and his prayers became more personal than ever before. He continued to battle cancer and give all he could to fight this dreadful disease. He spent time with Kristin and Matt and the rest of his family. About four months later, on March 28, Rod met the One who had whispered in his ears as he drove down the road. This time, rather than saying, "I've got this," I suspect God said, "I've got you."

The "What" of Holy Conversation

The initiating movement of all holy conversation begins with the God of the universe.

God speaks, we hear. Often we think that we are the initiators, but God is the sovereign ruler of all things. If he had not reached out to us first, we would never be able to find him. One of the joys of this reality is that God tends to speak in ways we can understand. For Rod, the words "I've got this" were perfect. That is just what Rod needed to hear. We should expect God to speak in ways we will understand. We should keep our ears open to anything God wants to say. When the prophet Eli taught little Samuel to pray, he instructed him to say, "Speak, LORD, your servant is listening" (1 Sam. 3:9). We would do well to pray in the same way.

We speak, God hears. Once we hear from God, we need to respond. If you hear a word of conviction from the Holy Spirit, respond with confession. Or ask, "What would you have me do? How should I change? How can I live differently and honor you?" Then listen for an answer. If you hear a word of blessing and encouragement from the Lord, thank him and ask for power to live more fully for his glory. Over and over we are assured that if we pray to God, he hears us (1 John 5:14; Psalm 66:17–20). This interplay of hearing and speaking can go back and forth many times, like any other conversation.

We obey, God is glorified. As God speaks to us and we respond, this should lead to life-transforming action. In the book of James we are told that we are not to simply hear the word of the Lord, but we are to be moved to action (James 1:22). Part of holy conversation is heart and life change. Our holy conversations with God should shape our attitudes, change our motives, launch us outward with compassionate action, drive us to our knees in confession, shape our character. Holy conversations lead to holy living.

Go to the Ends of the Earth

I experienced this exact process when the leader of the World Mission board said, "I really would like to see one of our board members join the team that will be doing our largest solar audio Bible distribution so far." As a member of the board, I saw the importance of this trip, but in my mind I did not think it would be the trip for me to go on. The trip included hand-delivering Treasures (audio Bibles) to remote peoples living in very small villages in the Himalayas. The trip would include long flights and rigorous living conditions, and no women had signed up for the portion of the trip in which we would be trekking the Himalayan Mountains for five days.

My dilemma was that I felt a strong conviction of the Holy Spirit as I walked out of that board meeting. I felt that I was to go on this trip. I knew God was speaking because I responded—I began to explain to God why I should not go on this trip. Over the years I have found that I often know God is talking to me because I notice I am talking back. This is usually a sign to step back and listen more closely.

I began to reason with God. I would be the only woman on this portion of the trip and Kevin was already committed to lead another mission trip, so he would be unable to accompany me. I had also gone through a complex neck surgery and was still in physical therapy and in a healing process. I gave my list to God as I tried to negotiate my way out of going.

Of course, God did not let up. The conviction and whispers continued for some time. The sense that I should go with the team to India and Nepal only grew. I spoke to God: "Lord, I am willing to go if this is your will. But I feel it would not be right for me to be the only woman on the trip and not have my husband there. Lord, open a door or change my heart."

A short time after that specific prayer, God answered this prayer. I was telling our oldest son, Zach, about the challenge I was facing. I explained my concerns and asked him to pray for me. He responded, "What if I go with you and the team?" A wave of Spirit-given peace came over me. I felt this was God's answer. I was to go on the trip.

God spoke and I listened. I spoke and God heard my concerns. God spoke and continued to call me. I mounted my reasons why it would not work. God provided a way. We had gone back and forth a number of times over several weeks before the answer came.

I went on the trip with the team and with my son. God was present and powerful. We saw pastors receive amazing resources, we shared the gospel, and we handed out hundreds of audio Bibles in the native languages that were represented. We watched as lives were changed for eternity. Zach and I were obedient to the call and God was glorified in powerful ways. This experience of trekking the Himalayas with the World Mission team and my son was powerful. We hiked for six hours each day, sleeping in unheated huts and at times using bathroom facilities that were essentially holes in the ground. The trip proved to be one of the best experiences of my life. Only God! I am so thankful I heard and followed his voice. This is holy conversation at its best. Always real, often messy, time-consuming, and life changing!

The Ultimate Holy Conversation

In the very beginning of the book of Hebrews, we discover what I have come to call the "Ultimate Holy Conversation."

Read these words slowly and let their power penetrate your soul:

> In the past God spoke to our ancestors through the prophets at many times and in various ways, but in these last days he has spoken to us by his Son, whom he appointed heir of all things, and through whom also he made the universe. The Son is the radiance of God's glory and the exact representation of his being, sustaining all things by his powerful word. After he had provided purification for sins, he sat down at the right hand of the Majesty in heaven. (Heb. 1:1–3)

God has spoken with clarity and power through his prophets. The Scriptures are the absolute and final revelation of God: unchanging, true, and Spirit-breathed. But in these last days, God has spoken to us through Jesus, the Christ, his only Son.

The ultimate conversation is the gospel. It is the Good News of Jesus Christ. The God of heaven has spoken through his only begotten Son. The message is clear: "But God demonstrates his own love for us in this: While we were still sinners, Christ died for us" (Rom. 5:8). Though we were lost in sin and condemned to death, God offered life through the sacrifice of Jesus, the Lamb of God who takes away the sins of the world (Rom. 3:23; 6:23; and John 1:29). Jesus, the Word of God, has spoken: "Come to me." We respond to his grace by faith alone and say, "Yes, Lord, I come" (Rom. 10:9–10). When we confess our sins and declare our trust in him, we are cleansed (1 John 1:9).

This is the ultimate holy conversation. God calls our name and offers his grace. We confess our sins and declare our faith. When this happens, a lost lamb is found (Luke 15:3–7), a wandering child comes home (Luke 15:11–27), and the angels of heaven rejoice (Luke 15:10). After this first conversation, the door is opened and we have full access to our Father through the work of Jesus as the Holy Spirit leads us. We can talk to God, and this begins a lifetime of holy conversations.

The Rest of the Story

On my first anniversary I was irritated with my husband because I did not have what he had. Kevin had been a Christian for only about six years and I had loved Jesus for almost two decades. I resented the fact that he seemed to have this close personal connection that I had missed.

We sat in that hotel room working through the theology of prayer and communication with God. I asked Kevin how he began entering into conversational prayer. His answer was simple and a bit humorous: "Before I became a Christian, I watched and listened to the people around me who were living for Jesus. They talked about Jesus like they knew him, like he was a friend, like Jesus actually loved them."

Then Kevin looked straight at me and said, "I believed them! So, when I received the grace of Jesus and his sacrifice on the cross, I just started praying to Jesus like a friend. I assumed a friend would not leave you hanging but would respond. And Jesus did respond. He still does, every day."

Now Kevin and I journey through life together, praying with our eyes wide open. It is not unusual for us to pray together five to ten times a day. We rarely stop what we are doing and say, "Let's pray." We close our eyes sometimes. But most of the time one of us just begins praying as we walk, talk, drive, eat, and do life together. Sometimes the other will join in. Our conversations with each other are infused with prayer. And our prayers are holy conversations.

For some of those reading this chapter, you might feel discouraged just like I did on my first anniversary. Maybe you really want to hear from God, but you are not feeling connected in a way that allows you to recognize his voice. Don't be disheartened. Keep praying, listening, and responding when God speaks through the Bible, through people, and through circumstances. Be faithful when God does speak, and keep listening. Remove mental clutter, ask God good questions, and be patient. God is ready to speak, but it will be in his timing.

Your Prayer Journey

Holy conversations are not complete until we take action on what God has spoken to us. God does speak. We respond to him. Humble obedience is the fruit of our holy conversations. Take time and reflect on some of the ways God has clearly spoken to you but you have not taken action. It could be a conversation where the Holy Spirit convicted you of sin, but you have still not repented and turned from a specific attitude or behavior. It could be a conversation when God called you to begin serving, giving more generously, or sharing your faith more boldly. You have heard from God but you have not yet responded. When you identify a way God has spoken and you have not yet acted, commit to take action. Pray for power. Tell a Christian friend what you plan to do so you have accountability. Confess to God that you have been holding back and invite your heavenly Father to move you forward in action that puts hands and feet to your prayers.

PRAYING WITH **HEARTS**

WIDE
OPEN

I pray that the *eyes of your heart* may be enlightened in order that you may know the hope to which he has called you, the riches of his glorious inheritance in his holy people, and his incomparably great power for us who believe. That power is the same as the mighty strength he exerted when he raised Christ from the dead and seated him at his right hand in the heavenly realms.

EPHESIANS 1:18–20 (EMPHASIS ADDED)

A heart open to God will help you see who he is and pray with greater passion and transparent honesty. A heart tuned in to God will alert you to the spiritual battles Christians face in our world today and lead you to victory over the enemy. When we open our heart to God in prayer, his peace fills us and anxiety runs for the back door and scurries away!

Nine

The Father Is Fond of You

This is love: not that we loved God, but that he loved us and
sent his Son as an atoning sacrifice for our sins.

1 JOHN 4:10

In a lifetime of data and learning, some lessons, pieces of information, and truths get missed. Important things simply get
passed over and never settle into our full awareness. My husband,
Kevin, is a bright man and a very serious student. When we
married, he had graduated from a great college and was doing
his master's degree. But there were strange gaps in his education
and knowledge base.

For instance, at that time he did not know how to read a map.
In particular, he did not know that when you look at a map, up
is north, down is south, right is east, and left is west. I thought
everyone knew that, but Kevin had missed it. In addition, he
hadn't learned a number of simple grammatical oddities, lessons

that I was teaching my second-grade class at the time—for example, the difference between *to* and *too*.

I am not seeking to be critical at all. I love my husband and respect his intelligence. But I was shocked to learn that a bright man in his early twenties had these gaps in his learning. Over the next couple of years, I taught him these things and other small lessons he had missed growing up.

A Massive Lesson Missed

It is nice to know that north on a map is upward. It is helpful to know that when using "too," you should be able to replace it with "also" or "excessively." But missing these things is not a spiritual tragedy. When I was in my early twenties, I discovered a lesson I had missed that was far more important than any of the things Kevin had overlooked.

I was raised by deeply devoted, loving, and sincere Christian parents. Their faith, then and now, is an example to me. I went to a Bible-preaching church Sunday mornings and Sunday evenings, and I was happy to go for the most part. I was often the last person to leave, because I loved Jesus and the people of God. I attended Sunday school with teachers who delighted to see children learn about Jesus and the Bible. I even attended midweek catechism classes and learned from them. All of this, and I still missed it!

I made a commitment to Jesus at five years old. I believed the Bible was true and the very Word of God. I read my Bible and did daily devotions. I attended Calvin College, a top academic school that took the Christian faith very seriously. I was immersed in a vibrant faith community and an extended family that loved Jesus. With all of this, and the flood of great biblical teaching filling my mind and heart, I have to humbly admit, I missed one of the most important lessons in the Bible. Sadly, I did not realize I had missed this truth until I was in my early twenties.

A Life-Changing Revelation

Early in our ministry I went to a leadership conference with my husband. We were serving a church in Glendora, California, and part of our training was ongoing education. On the second day of the event, we heard that one of the main speakers had to pull out of the event and he would not be coming to speak. Instead, a man named Brennan Manning would be filling in for him. We had never heard of Brennan, but God was about to use this man to teach me a truth that had eluded me for two decades.

Brennan was a passionate, quirky, wiry man who spoke from the depth of his heart in a way I had seldom heard. His message was about the relentless grace of God. He was committed to helping all of us understand that God is a loving *Abba* who cares more about us than we could imagine or dream.

In his message, he told a simple story that became a key to unlock my heart and allow me to receive a gift I had not yet fully understood or embraced. Brennan related an account of a priest named Edward Farrell from Detroit, Michigan, who went to Ireland to celebrate the eightieth birthday of his uncle Seamus. Early on the morning of the great day, Edward and his uncle went for a long walk along the shores of Lake Killarney. As the sun crept up and warmed the earth, his uncle stood still and gazed into the morning light for almost twenty minutes, saying nothing.

Then, unexpectedly, Uncle Seamus began to skip along the shore of Lake Killarney, his face radiant with a smile from ear to ear. When Edward Farrell caught up with his uncle, he said, "Uncle Seamus, you look very happy. Do you want to tell me why?"

"Yes, lad," Uncle Seamus said, his face beaming even brighter and tears streaming down his cheeks. "You see, me Abba is very fond of me."[1]

As I sat listening, tears began to roll down my face. They were tears of wonder, sorrow, and joy all mingled together. I realized that I had missed it. I could tell you that God loved me, I could quote Bible verses to support this fact, and I actually believed it! But I did not know that God was fond of me . . . that he liked me. I had not skipped in sheer joy because of the deep and personal awareness that the God of the universe delighted in me. I had never stood in awestruck wonder at the reality that I am a beloved and cherished daughter of God.

In that moment my tears were partly for what I had missed, but more than that, they were for the gift of what I had just found. This was a truth that must have been taught to me many times, but it had never sunk in. My husband had missed the lesson on how to use *to* or *too*. I had missed the heart of the gospel that I received as a five-year-old child. I had not recognized that I was God's beloved.

From that day on, everything would begin to change. When my heart was captured by this truth, my prayer life began to change in beautiful and glorious ways.

God Loves Us and He Likes Us

The apostle Paul went through a process of discovering the love and delight of God. Though he had been a hater of the church and a persecutor of Christians, Paul received God's amazing grace and was transformed. When our hearts open to receive the truth of God's delight over us, we are compelled to communicate with this God. Listen to the passion of Paul's prayer:

> For this reason I kneel before the Father, from whom every family in heaven and on earth derives its name. I pray that out of his glorious riches he may strengthen you with power through his Spirit in your inner being, so that Christ may dwell in your hearts through faith. And I pray that you, being rooted and established in love, may have power, together with all the Lord's holy people, to grasp how wide and long and high and deep is the love of Christ, and to know this love that surpasses knowledge—that you may be filled to the measure of all the fullness of God. (Eph. 3:14–19)

Paul fell on his knees in praise for God's fatherly love. He lifted up supplication for the people of God. His deep desire was that followers of Jesus would grasp the greatness of God's love. The language he used is striking. How wide, long, high, and deep is this love of God. It is a love beyond measure. It surpasses knowledge. It is as if Paul was saying, "May you comprehend the massive nature of God's love for you, a love that can never be fully understood."

When I began to realize that God not only loves me, he also likes me, my understanding of God grew. So did my awareness of who I am. I am a loved and cherished child of the Ruler of the universe. God is my *Abba*. This continues to transform my prayer life in four distinct ways:

1. *I pray knowing that God is radically approachable.* When I realized that God likes me, I began to believe that he likes being with me. I can enter his presence with confidence that his arms are wide open. I remember that while Jesus was hanging on the cross, bearing my sins and paying the

price for my rebellion, the curtain in the temple was torn in two from top to bottom (Matt. 27:51). It was as if the very hands of God gripped the curtain and ripped it in half. This physical divider was the visual reminder that only the high priest could enter the most holy place, and then only once a year, to offer a blood sacrifice. This curtain was a symbol of separation. When Jesus offered salvation and grace as he died on the cross, the curtain was torn and the approach to the very presence of God was opened for all of his children.

2. *I pray with growing hunger for an intimate relationship with him.* When I am confident that God loves me and likes me, I seek a closer friendship with my Creator. I am not drawn to people who don't like me. I am drawn to those who care about me. As I understand that the Father is fond of me, I hunger for a deeper relationship with him.

3. *I pray feeling free to be who I am*, even in my brokenness. I don't have to pretend or put on a show for someone who loves me and likes me. I am free to be myself. What I have learned over the years is that this freedom to be who I am releases me to become who God would have me be.

4. *I pray and my fears evaporate.* Life is full of fear—fear of rejection, judgment, abandonment, and countless other things. When I live with a clear vision of how God sees me, fear runs for the back door and heads out of town. I am not talking about awe for God's glory or even a holy fear of the Almighty God of the universe. I am talking about unreasonable fears that drive me away from God. I am talking about ungodly fears instilled by the enemy.

When I embrace the perfect love of God, fear disappears like morning mist as the sun rises. The Bible teaches that "there is no fear in love. But perfect love drives out fear, because fear has to do with punishment. The one who fears is not made perfect in love" (1 John 4:18).

The love of God for you and me is so great that the only picture that comes close to reflecting God's heart is his beloved Son hanging on a cruel cross, bearing our sin and shame and offering us his righteousness (2 Cor. 5:21). No matter how much we think we understand this gift and comprehend God's love, there is still more to learn. There is more to be received. There is always more!

A Right View of God

Our view of God affects every aspect of our life and faith. The great pastor and theologian A. W. Tozer penned these words:

> What comes into our mind when we think about God is the most important thing about us. . . . Were we able to extract from any man a complete answer to the question, "What comes into your mind when you think about God?" we might predict with certainty the spiritual future of that man.[2]

If we view God as disinterested, we will not draw near him. If we view God as a kind but weak old man in the sky, we will not trust him to deliver in times of need. If we believe God is an angry judge looking for a reason to throw the book at us, we will run away and hide from him. But when we know that God loves us and is fond of us, we run to his arms with deep trust and confidence that he wants the best for us. This leads to prayer at all times and in all places.

God's Love for the World

In the Gospel of John, right after Jesus' encounter with Nicodemus, we read these words:

> For God so loved the world that he gave his one and only Son, that whoever believes in him shall not perish but have eternal life. For God did not send his Son into the world to condemn the world, but to save the world through him. Whoever believes in him is not condemned, but whoever does not believe stands condemned already because they have not believed in the name of God's one and only Son. (John 3:16–18)

God's love extends beyond those who are already in the church and part of his family. God's love is big enough for the whole world.

Kevin and I have spent over thirty years serving the local church. We have also spent these years training and helping other churches, denominational leaders, and international leaders as they seek to be outwardly focused and develop a culture of evangelistic faithfulness. We use the term "Organic Outreach" (see organicoutreach.com). This is the practice of sharing God's love and good news naturally. We believe that God's heart for the world should move our hearts to action. We believe God's love for the world should move us to passionate and persistent prayers for those who are still far from Jesus.

Henry's Story

Deb was the last of five children born to Henry and Betty. She grew up in a caring family that had no Christian faith. Her father, Henry, was a farmer and loved to share his produce with friends and neighbors. Deb loved her family and felt very loved by her parents.

When Deb met Bruce, they fell in love, got married, and started their own family. Bruce was a Christian, and Deb soon discovered the love and grace of Jesus. She received the Savior, joined a local church, and began growing in her newfound faith. When she told her father she had become a Christian, she thought he would be happy for her. Instead, he said, "You can do what you want, but I think you are making a mistake."

These words broke her heart and motivated her to begin praying for her father. Months and years passed and Henry showed no sign of opening his heart to God's love and grace. Deb would find herself wondering, "Why am I trying so hard and praying so much? It does not seem to be making a difference." Instead of giving up, she committed to keep praying and invite others to pray for her dad also. About two decades into her prayer journey, as Deb shared her heart for her dad, I made a commitment to pray for my dear friend's father. Deb also opened the door for Kevin to visit her dad and build a friendship.

Over the next decade Kevin developed a relationship with Henry and visited him on occasion. I made a commitment to Deb that I would pray for her dad every time I drove past his house, which was about a dozen times every week. I told Deb that I would do my best to let his home remind me to pray for him. Through the years Henry showed no signs of softening his heart, but we kept praying and loving him. We all knew that Jesus loved Henry, and we longed to see him embrace the amazing grace of the Savior.

When Henry was in his late eighties, they found out he had bone cancer. It was advanced and the doctors were clear that Henry did not have much more time on this earth. Deb kept praying and cried out to the Lord to send medical professionals who loved Jesus and who would add their voices to the others who were sharing the gospel with Henry. In the coming days many prayed, and one of the medical helpers did share the story of Jesus with Henry, but all outward appearance made it clear that he was not interested.

After a long day at the hospital, with a report from the doctor that Henry's condition was growing worse and he did not have much more time, Deb took her mom home to sleep and stayed with her for the night. All those who knew Deb increased their prayers, along with Deb. She prayed late into the night, lifting up honest prayers and shedding many tears.

About four in the morning, Deb woke up to the sound of bells ringing. She walked around the living room, trying to figure out where this beautiful music was coming from, and concluded it must be from the clock in the living room. When Deb's mom woke up, Deb asked her about the clock and the beautiful music it played, but her mom assured her the clock was broken and had not been working for years.

A short time later they headed to the hospital to visit Henry. When Deb walked into the room, she was shocked when she saw tears streaming down her father's face. He had an uncommon radiance to his countenance, and he said, "Debbie, come over here. I have to tell you something. I know you will understand." Deb came close and looked into his face. Henry said, "You don't have to worry anymore. I met Jesus. He came to me today." Deb was overjoyed and breathless. Later, as she reflected on the bells and music she had heard that morning, she concluded that God, in his grace and mercy, had allowed her to know the moment that her earthly father met Jesus. In the last days of his life, Henry met Jesus and discovered that the Father was fond of him. Henry lived for a little over a week after that precious morning and then went home to his loving heavenly Father.

I still remember the first time I drove by Henry's house after he passed away. I reflexively wanted to pray, since I had done it so many times over the previous years. Instead of my regular prayer for Henry, I simply praised the Father for his love and grace. I also thanked God for the privilege of sharing in Henry's journey through praying with my eyes wide open as I drove by his house. As best I can tell, I prayed for Henry's heart to soften and receive the Father's love through Jesus over a dozen times each week for nine years. His daughter Deb had prayed far more than that—she had prayed for her father for over thirty years. When you add the prayers of all Deb's family and friends, the number of prayers is staggering. As I drove by, I thought how much God must love Henry to move so many people to pray for him all those years, including me, a person who did not know him and never met him. It was truly God's love for Henry that moved me to pray all those years. This is the heart of the Father. Our prayers were a small reflection of the greatness of God's love.

Drive-By Prayers

In the coming months Deb talked to me about how she began praying as she drove by other people's homes. She shared how my example of praying for her father with my eyes wide open had inspired her to do what she now calls "drive-by prayers."

Imagine what could happen if every Christian developed a habit of doing drive-by prayers. Christians would pray more for people they know—and like in my case with Henry, some they don't even know—as they drive by different reminder points.

Maybe God's Spirit would stir you to start praying for local churches. Whenever you drive or pass by a church, you would pray for God's blessings, for a great work of the Holy Spirit among that fellowship of believers, and for that local church to love and serve their community by sharing the grace of Jesus in natural ways. What might God do through those prayers?

Police and firefighters would be lifted up and prayers for protection and wisdom would be lavished on them as the Holy Spirit reminded believers to pray as they drive by their local police station or firehouse. Civic leaders would be covered in prayer as believers drive by and ask God to bless those in places of community leadership and influence. You might be moved to lift up prayers for schools, teachers, administrators, and students each time you drive by a place of education. As Christians drive and pray with their eyes open, power would be unleashed and lives would be changed.

When we realize, in the core of our being, that the Father is fond of us, we recognize that he is also fond of the people we encounter each day. We take delight in knowing that we are loved and liked. And we are moved to love, serve, and pray for the people God brings across our path each day.

I pray that if I live to be eighty years old, someone will look at me and ask, "Why do you look so happy?" If they do, I will say, "You see, me Abba is very fond of me. My Father is so very fond of me." But more than this, I hope I can tell people this truth every day of my life. It is my prayer that you also will know that the Father is fond of you, which seems to be a good reason to skip and smile.

Your Prayer Journey

When you know the Father is fond of you, you discover that he is fond of others. Identify one person you know who lives near you and who is not yet a follower of Jesus. Commit to pray for this person each time you go by their home. Ask for God to open their heart and eyes to his grace. Pray for courage and opportunities to share God's love and message of grace with this person. Take a walk with the God who loves you. Spend the entire time on your walk asking God to help you understand how fond he is of you. If you have a sense that he loves you and likes you, feel free to skip! If someone asks you why you are skipping, you know what to tell them: "The Father is fond of me!"

Ten

Honest to God

It is of great importance, when we begin to practice prayer, not
to let ourselves be frightened by our own thoughts.

TERESA OF ÁVILA

Can we be totally honest with God in prayer? Should we be?
I believe the answer to both of these questions is a bold "Yes!"
For many years I was confused about this topic. I can't identify
exactly where it came from, but I had a sense that it might be
disrespectful or dishonoring to tell God everything that was on
my heart. Being well aware of my own sinfulness and brokenness caused me to hold back and not pray with unrestrained
transparency.

It was my love for the book of Psalms that brought me to
a place of breakthrough. As I immersed myself in these biblical prayers, the Holy Spirit gave me insight, clarity, and fresh
conviction that honest prayers are not only allowed, but they
please God. Throughout the Psalms, I heard other passionate

followers of God bring their pain, fear, anger, and struggles into the presence of the Lord of glory. These prayers struck me as raw, vulnerable, fear-filled, shocking at times, and encouraging.

As I began praying the psalms and letting these ancient songs pray for me, honesty began to feel natural. Rather than being irreverent, my truthful prayers felt God-honoring. Instead of creating a sense of guilt, they freed me to pour out my heart and discover new depths of grace.

Out of the Depths

On my journey toward honest prayer, I was introduced to a book simply titled *Out of the Depths*. In this insightful book, Bernhard W. Anderson introduces the psalms of lament and the form of the laments. This is a group of psalms that are cries from the depths of pain, loss, fear, brokenness, and despair. I had been praying these psalms and letting them pray for me, but I was unaware that there was a specific kind of prayer titled "lament." I did not know that many others had walked this same road of discovery and had grown to love these prayers and hold on to them in their hard times.

Dietrich Bonhoeffer, the martyred Christian pastor who resisted the Nazi regime, had a deep love for the psalms. He regarded the book of Psalms as his favorite book in the Bible. These prayers would have been on his heart and lips as he suffered in the Flossenbürg concentration camp and finally as he was executed because of his faith and dissent. His last publication before his execution was *The Prayer Book of the Bible: An Introduction to the Psalms* (1940). In this writing he developed the idea that just as Jesus Christ has taught us to pray the words of the Lord's Prayer, the book of Psalms, "the prayer book of the Bible," guides and instructs us in greater fullness the words that God wants us to speak to him in the name of Jesus Christ.[1] I became aware that I was part of a community of Christians who let the psalms become both an instructor and a friend in the furnace of life.

As I learned from Anderson, Bonhoeffer, and others, a fresh picture formed in my mind. God not only welcomes prayers of lament, he gave them to us to affirm that there will be times when prayers like this will spill from our hearts and lips.

Just before the first verse of Psalm 102, there is a simple and telling superscription: "A prayer of an afflicted person who has grown weak and pours out a lament before the LORD." Wow, what an introduction! What follows are raw, honest, tear-streaked words:

> Hear my prayer, LORD;
>> let my cry for help come to you.
> Do not hide your face from me
>> when I am in distress.
> Turn your ear to me;
>> when I call, answer me quickly.
>
> For my days vanish like smoke;
>> my bones burn like glowing embers.
> My heart is blighted and withered like grass;
>> I forget to eat my food.
> In my distress I groan aloud
>> and am reduced to skin and bones.
> I am like a desert owl,
>> like an owl among the ruins.
> I lie awake; I have become
>> like a bird alone on a roof.
> All day long my enemies taunt me;
>> those who rail against me use my name as a curse.

For I eat ashes as my food
and mingle my drink with tears. (vv. 1–9)

The lesson I am still learning is that, at its core, prayer is an honest conversation with the God who is absolute truth. When our prayers lack honesty, they lack power. Praying with an open heart means recognizing that God already sees everything. Even what we wish was hidden. This frees us to express ourselves with intentional transparency because we know that God is sovereign and omniscient. He knows everything about us and he still loves us.

A Structure and a Flow

As I learned more about the psalms of lament, I found that there are many groups or types of psalms in the Bible. Some of these are Thanksgiving Psalms, Wisdom Psalms, Royal Psalms (about the king), Messianic Psalms (pointing to the Messiah, Jesus), Psalms of Ascent (to be sung while going on pilgrimage to Jerusalem), and Psalms of Lament. Of all the categories of psalms, the largest grouping is actually the laments; more than one-third of all the psalms are lament psalms. Not only are these the most common, but there is a consistent structure that most of the laments follow. As I learned this flow of prayer within the laments, it began to help shape my honest prayers in times of sorrow, loss, and struggle. Not every lament psalm follows this pattern exactly, but the general flow goes like this:

1. **Address to God**—Calling out to God using one of his names or attributes.
2. **Honest and heartfelt complaint**—Whatever you are facing: sickness, fear of enemies, awareness of sin, physical

pain, relational brokenness, heartache . . . poured out with shocking truthfulness.

3. **Confession of trust in God**—A bold declaration that God is still powerful and present no matter what we face.

4. **Petition for needs**—An honest cry for help in the midst of the storm and a plea for strength to overcome.

5. **Words of assurance**—An expression of trust that this prayer is being heard by God Almighty.

6. **Vow of praise**—A confident declaration of continued praise and worship.[2]

Even with a quick and simple review of these six movements of prayer, we can begin to see the beauty of how God is teaching us to pray from the heart. The flow matches a heart that loves and trusts God but is also being ravaged by the storms of life.

A prayer of lament begins as a man or woman cries out to God. Because there is a relationship, there is some form of direct address. "Hear my prayer, LORD" (Ps. 102:1) and "My God, my God" (Ps. 22:1) are examples of this natural address. Prayer is speaking to God; so calling out one of his names is appropriate and part of the structure of a lament.

Next, and often the largest part of the prayer, is honest complaint. Expressions of sorrow, pain, fear, frustration, and even anger are poured out with candid and passionate words. As we saw in Psalm 102, this can range from physical pain, to loneliness, to fear of enemies, to sadness. All of these are expressed in the same psalm in the portion called the complaint.

In the midst of this candid expression of pain and sorrow, there is almost always a point when the person praying pauses and declares deep trust and confidence in God. Though they are in pain and feeling broken, they still live with an abiding certainty that God is God, he is on the throne, and he can be trusted... no matter what. In Psalm 102, right after crying out, "My days are like the evening shadow; I wither away like grass," the psalmist declares, "But you, LORD, sit enthroned forever; your renown endures through all generations" (vv. 11–12). As we learn to be honest to God in prayer, it is critical that we declare our trust and confidence, even as we pour out our struggles and pain.

Since we are praying to the God who is able to do all things, it is natural, even when honestly expressing struggle, to ask him for help. This is why psalms of lament almost always move into a time of humble and honest petition. If the person praying has lamented the attacks of an enemy, there is often a prayer for victory over that foe. If it is sickness or physical torment, a prayer for healing follows. If the complaint is the battle with sin, power for repentance and turning around is sought. Whatever the lament might be, a prayer for the situation to change should flow naturally from our heart and lips.

Finally, the person praying declares something like, "I will declare your name to my people; in the assembly I will praise you" (Ps. 22:22). Before finishing a prayer of lament, our trust and confidence in God's goodness and worthiness compel us to express our assurance that our prayers are being heard and that we will continue to praise him.

These six elements in a lament prayer are often found in this exact order: address, complaint, trust, petition, assurance, and praise. Sometimes an element can be missing. At other times the order can be slightly different. There are even times a prayer in the psalms might cycle back to complaint, praise, or an expression of need more than once. The point is not that an exact order needs to be followed. What we realize is that when our heart enters God's presence, our expressions of honest pain, declarations of continued trust, cries for help, and commitment to praise God, even in the greatest storms of life, flow from the depths of our soul to the God who welcomes these rugged and raw expressions of honest prayer. When we pray this way, we join the ancients in God-honoring lament and profoundly transparent prayer.

Confusion, Complaint, and Clarity

In Psalm 73 we have a beautiful opportunity to peek into the heart and journey of a passionate person of prayer. Through this prayer of Asaph, we discover that honesty in prayer leads to clarity of thought and a confident heart. Too often we seek to live our days guided by our own wisdom and understanding. In the third chapter of Proverbs we are warned not to trust in our own understanding: "Trust in the LORD with all your heart and lean not on your own understanding; in all your ways submit to him, and he will make your paths straight" (vv. 5–6). Honest prayer can actually crystallize our thinking and teach us to trust God at deeper levels.

The prayer in Psalm 73 begins with a declaration of belief: "Surely God is good to Israel, to those who are pure in heart" (v. 1). This is a confident proclamation. On the heels of this comes an emotional expression of what the psalmist is feeling: "But as for me, my feet had almost slipped; I had nearly lost my foothold. For I envied the arrogant when I saw the prosperity of the wicked" (vv. 2–3). He goes on to reflect on the wicked and arrogant and observes that they seem to prosper and get away with their evil practices (vv. 4–12). There is a sense of honest despair and a heavy heart about the injustice of people who walk far from God, rebel against the Lord, and still seem to come up smelling like roses.

The psalmist is confused and complaining. The world does not make sense. His observations and insight can't sort things out. His frustration culminates in the expression, "When I tried to understand all this, it troubled me deeply" (v. 16). With honest words and a transparent heart, he tells God that the world does not make sense.

The turning point of this psalmist's spiritual journey comes when he draws near to God, as seen in verse 17: "till I entered the sanctuary of God; then I understood their final destiny." Truth breaks through. His eyes are opened to the true fate of the wicked (vv. 18–20). Assurance floods in, hope is reborn, clarity is found in honest prayer. With his final words the writer declares, "But as for me, it is good to be near God. I have made the Sovereign Lord my refuge; I will tell of all your deeds" (v. 28). You can feel the peace of God calming the psalmist's heart as his confidence is bolstered.

When we face confusion and turmoil over the injustice of the world and the growth of evil around us, the answer is not to try to figure everything out in our own understanding. We should bring our frustrations and pain to God with bold confession of our inability to make sense of things. As we do this with humble honesty, God brings the clarity we can't attain on our own. As we draw near God in prayer, he gently pulls back the veil that covers our eyes and heart and shows us his glory, his power, his presence, and his plan.

God Invites Us to Come with Honest Prayers

Over and over God extends an invitation to draw near him as we are, with authentic prayers, even when we are hurting and confused. Read these passages slowly and reflectively. Hear the invitation God extends for you to come and speak your heart with boldness:

Psalm 91:14–16

> "Because he loves me," says the LORD, "I will rescue
> him;
> I will protect him, for he acknowledges my name.
> He will call on me, and I will answer him;
> I will be with him in trouble,
> I will deliver him and honor him.
> With long life I will satisfy him
> and show him my salvation."

Psalm 116:1–4

> I love the LORD, for he heard my voice;
> he heard my cry for mercy.
> Because he turned his ear to me,
> I will call on him as long as I live.
>
> The cords of death entangled me,
> the anguish of the grave came over me;
> I was overcome by distress and sorrow.
> Then I called on the name of the LORD:
> "LORD, save me!"

Psalm 145:18–19

> The LORD is near to all who call on him,
> to all who call on him in truth.
> He fulfills the desires of those who fear him;
> he hears their cry and saves them.

Isaiah 55:1, 3

> Come, all you who are thirsty,
> come to the waters;
> and you who have no money,
> come, buy and eat!
> Come, buy wine and milk
> without money and without cost. . . .

Give ear and come to me;
 listen, that you may live.
I will make an everlasting covenant with you,
 my faithful love promised to David.

Jeremiah 33:3
 Call to me and I will answer you and tell you great and un-
searchable things you do not know.

Micah 7:7
 But as for me, I watch in hope for the LORD,
 I wait for God my Savior;
 my God will hear me.

While some may think God does not tolerate our prayers from the depths of our sorrow, confusion, and pain, he actually invites them. He waits for them. He hears these prayers because he loves us.

Jesus Modeled Honest Prayers of Lament

When Jesus was hanging on the cross bearing our sins and taking our shame, he prayed. In his hour of need and sorrow, Jesus quoted a lament psalm and made it his own. Our Savior pierced the sky as he cried out, "My God, my God, why have you forsaken me?" (Ps. 22:1). Every Jewish person on the hill of Golgotha would have recognized these words inspired through King David a thousand years earlier. Jesus went to the prayer book of God's people and let the words become his own.

If you have any worry about being honest with God and letting the psalms of lament become part of your prayer life, worry no longer. Jesus shows us the way forward on our spiritual journey, and the Savior gave us an example of honest prayer as he offered his own life and blood to open the way for us to be saved and come home to the Father.

God Can Handle Your Honesty

Maybe you were raised to believe it is irreverent, undignified, or even ungodly to be entirely honest with God in prayer. In his book *You'll Get Through It*, Max Lucado gives this advice for Christians who are walking through a time of great pain, struggle, and confusion: "Pray your pain out. Pound the table. March up and down the lawn. It's time for tenacious, honest prayers. Angry at God? Disappointed at his strategy? Ticked off at his choices? Let him know it."[3] I love this challenge and I have been learning to live it out. I am discovering that the more honest I am, the more vibrant my prayer life becomes. The more transparent I become, the more intimate I feel with my God.

Stop and think about what we are saying when we lock up our frustration and swallow our sorrow. We are acting like God can't handle our honest expressions of pain and anger. We are pretending that God does not know. But God searches our hearts and nothing is hidden from his eyes. God knows everything about us, even what we try to hide.

In Psalm 139 David reflects on what God knows about us. God searches us and sees everything. He knows our actions, thoughts, and words. The Maker of the universe even knows the words we choose not to say: "Before a word is on my tongue you, LORD, know it completely" (v. 4). There is no place in all creation where God is not present. Even in the womb of our mother, God was there, intimately making us and caring for us. God knows every day of our life, before even one transpires. Since God knows everything, let's not hold back. It is time to start praying with new levels of honesty and frankness.

Pouring Out, Not Pouring In!

One of my favorite women in the Bible is Hannah. We meet this great woman of faith and hear her story in the first two chapters of 1 Samuel. She has suffered with barrenness for at least a decade. In a culture where having children was seen as a blessing, Hannah felt dejected and forgotten by God. In the depths of sorrow she came into the house of God in Shiloh. Out of a place of deep trouble and heartache, she prayed and cried out to God. Her suffering was so profound that she had no words, but she moved her lips and poured out her heart to God.

What happened next only compounded her sorrow. The priest, Eli, accused her of being drunk. Her heart was so broken and her behavior so severe, the elderly priest assumed she was under the influence: "How long are you going to stay drunk? Put away your wine" (1:14). Hannah's response is an example for all of us: "'Not so, my lord,' Hannah replied, 'I am a woman who is deeply troubled. I have not been drinking wine or beer; I was pouring out my soul to the LORD. Do not take your servant for a wicked woman; I have been praying here out of my great anguish and grief'" (1:15–16). She corrects the great Eli and explains that she is pouring out, not pouring in. In times of pain, loss, and suffering, these seem to be the two common and opposite responses.

We can seek to medicate our hurt, confusion, and shattered heart by pouring in drink, drugs, food, shopping, work, or other things intended to numb our heart. Or we can pour out our heart with honest prayer. We can come before God and tell him exactly what we are feeling. We can admit our fear, uncover our shame, express our anger, and open our heart to the God who already knows everything about us and has proven his unending love through the ultimate sacrifice, his own life.

If being honest to God has not been a part of your prayer life or is an area that needs to be developed, it is my prayer that you will let the Scriptures speak for you and direct you as you continue on this journey of learning how to pray with your heart wide open to God.

Your Prayer Journey

Use the simple structure of a Lament Psalm and pray your own lament to God. Be as honest as you can and be sure to declare your trust as well as your pain and struggles. Ask God to show you what you tend to pour into yourself when you should be pouring out your sorrow and heartache to God. Pray for power to stop pouring in when you should be pouring out.

Eleven

Warfare Prayers

God's child can conquer everything by prayer. Is it any wonder
that Satan does his utmost to snatch that weapon from the
Christian or to hinder him in the use of it?

ANDREW MURRAY

My firstborn son, Zach, was heading off to full days of school
for the first time. He would get on a bus and head out, away
from my care, away from my sight, away from my protection
and motherly love . . . but not away from my prayers. I needed
to go deeper in prayer and trust God with greater intensity as I
released my son for the better part of a day. I was drawn to read
John 17, Jesus's High Priestly Prayer. I wanted to learn from the
Master. I hungered to know how to pray for those I love the
most, and this portion of the Bible is where Jesus prays for his
beloved disciples.

I had read John 17 many times through my years of following
Jesus, but this time the context and unique setting of my life

presented a fresh opening that the wind of God's Spirit could blow through.

Shortly after this prayer, Jesus would die on the cross. He would bear our sins and conquer death. He would take his last breath, be placed in a tomb for three days, and be raised in power. After a time of teaching and ministry, he would ascend to the Father. His disciples, his followers, his spiritual children would not have him with them day in and day out. Yes, Jesus would send the Holy Spirit to be with and in them. But he would not be physically present to walk with them. With this reality in mind, Jesus prayed for them.

As a mother facing this new reality in my life—my children out of the shadow of my motherly wings—I learned to pray in new ways that have changed my life. As I read this powerful prayer of the Savior, it struck me that this is a spiritual warfare prayer. I had never read it this way before. Here are the verses that gripped my heart, opened my eyes, and transformed my prayer life:

> I will remain in the world no longer, but they are still in the world, and I am coming to you. Holy Father, protect them by the power of your name, the name you gave me, so that they may be one as we are one. While I was with them, I protected them and kept them safe by that name you gave me. . . . My prayer is not that you take them out of the world but that you protect them from the evil one. They are not of the world, even as I am not of it. (John 17:11–12, 15–16)

Jesus cried out for his spiritual children. He would not be with them, but the power of the Father is always enough to protect and save. Jesus knew they would be in the world, so he prayed for protection from the Evil One. This truth began to shape practices of prayer that remain with me over two decades later.

Protection Prayers

Zach was in first grade. Josh and Nate were preschoolers. As they moved out of my circle of protection, I prayed more. Later I would go even deeper. When all three were off to school, sporting events, and overnight times with friends, I would pray, "Holy God, in the power of the name of Jesus, protect my boys. They do not belong to this world. They are yours. I do not pray that you remove them from this world; it is my prayer that your light shines through them in the darkness of the world they live in. I do pray that you protect them from the Evil One, the prince of this world" (see John 12:31). This practice of protection prayers took on new dimensions and intensity when they started driving, when they went off to college, and even now, as they have all become adults.

As my sons were growing up, I had a sense that my nurturing mother role changed with each new season. I had to work on lessening those mothering tendencies and loosening my grip. But there was one area I found my attention and intention could increase as they grew older: my prayer life for them. This piece of our relationship didn't need to decrease but instead could grow with the passing years.

The prayer of Jesus for his disciples has shaped my prayer life. There is rarely a day that Kevin and I do not pray together for each of our boys and now their wives. We pray like Jesus did, "Lord, we do not pray for you to take them from the world, we believe you have called them to shine their light while in this world, but protect them from the enemy in the power of your glorious name."

As I look back now, I realize my practice of praying for them as young children revealed something about my faith. I had a sense that when they were near me, I did not have to pray as intensely and passionately. I believed that I could protect them and meet their needs. Now I know that only God's grace is enough to keep my sons, my husband, my extended family and friends, and any person safe. Only God's power is sufficient.

Now I begin my day on my knees. As I roll out of bed and onto my knees, I pray for God's presence and power to protect me, my family, and those I love. I believe one of the greatest signs of true love is praying for people like Jesus prayed for his disciples in his longest prayer recorded in the Bible.

Here Is the Bad News

The whole human family can be broken into two groups of people when it comes to personal preferences of hearing good and bad news. Those who want to hear the bad news first are one group and those who want to hear the good news first are the other group. When it comes to this enduring debate, I am in the former group. If you ask me, "Do you want to hear the good news or the bad news first?" I will say, "Give me the bad news." I just want to get it over with.

So, here is the bad news: *You have an enemy!*

This enemy has many names: Satan, the devil, thief, and tempter, just to name a handful. Peter tells us that our enemy "prowls around like a roaring lion looking for someone to devour" (1 Pet. 5:8). Your enemy is real and he wants to destroy your life. He is deceitful, active, perpetually looking for a point of attack. He does not simply want to nibble on the edges of your life, he wants to swallow you whole and devour you.

Jesus tells us that the enemy of your soul is a "thief [who] comes only to steal and kill and destroy" (John 10:10). Satan wants to rob you of all that is good and beautiful. He is a killer from the beginning. He delights to destroy all the good things God has created. Don't let anyone give you the false impression that the devil has some people he likes and favors. The enemy only hates, kills, destroys, and deceives. There is no good in him.

Did you realize there is a being in this universe who is alive and actively seeking to "steal and kill and destroy"? Some people say Satan is alive and well. I say he is alive, but he is not well! He is dead set against you being spiritually alive and thriving in the power of God. You bear the image of the almighty Ruler of the universe. You carry the message of the gospel in your heart and on your lips. Because of this, the enemy hates you. He can do nothing to destroy your position and identity in Christ. But he will relentlessly seek to distract, deceive, and tempt you.

This is why we must pray. We make a tenacious choice to be people of prayer at all times, in all places, with our eyes wide open. There is a real enemy, but there is also a victorious weapon called prayer. Your prayers unleash the power of heaven.

Here Is the Good News

When Jesus was getting ready to leave this world, he prayed for protection of his children against the enemy. He sent the Holy Spirit to be in us and with us (John 14:15–21). God's Word assures us that "the one who is in you is greater than the one who is in the world" (1 John 4:4). We have power to resist temptation, fight the enemy, and walk in victory. Jesus came to give us life, and life to the fullest (John 10:10)!

Jesus himself prayed for his followers to be protected from the enemy. This should assure us that our enemy is real but the victory has already been won. Jesus conquered sin and the devil and invites us to enter the battle. Though God has won, we still need to stand strong and resist the enemy's enticements, reject his lies, and walk in the power of Jesus. Prayer becomes one of the weapons for the battle.

A Powerful Example and Exhortation

Patrice is a friend and a spiritual mentor. She has traveled down the road of faith a few decades farther than me. Patrice actually sang with Bob Hope on the USO tours during the Korean War. She has held the hand of Jesus as three husbands have passed away. She is a person of perpetual joy, constant grace, and tenacious faith-filled prayer.

In one of our conversations Patrice encouraged me to begin each day reading Ephesians 6:10–18 just as she has done for years. I have taken her advice. For the past few years I have started my day on my knees praying, and then I open my Bible and read these challenging words:

> Finally, be strong in the Lord and in his mighty power. Put on the full armor of God, so that you can take your stand against the devil's schemes. For our struggle is not against flesh and blood, but against the rulers, against the authorities, against the powers of this dark world and against the spiritual forces of evil in the heavenly realms. Therefore put on the full armor of God, so that when the day of evil comes, you may be able to stand your ground, and after you have done everything, to stand. Stand firm then, with the belt of truth buckled around your waist, with the breastplate of righteousness in place, and with your feet fitted with the readiness that comes from the gospel of peace. In addition to all this, take up the shield of faith, with which you can extinguish all the flaming arrows of the evil one. Take the helmet of salvation and the sword of the Spirit, which is the word of God.
>
> And pray in the Spirit on all occasions with all kinds of prayers and requests. With this in mind, be alert and always keep on praying for all the Lord's people.

I have not tired of this spiritual discipline. Each morning the Holy Spirit of God reminds me that walking into our world is an invitation to battle. These words of Scripture make me intentionally mindful of the enemy, the armor I must put on, and the absolute promise that God will help me stand, no matter what I face. I do not have to succumb to defeat. I can walk in victory and so can you.

As I have read, studied, and meditated on these words from Ephesians 6, a singular reality has gripped my soul and pierced my life: *The battle is real and the enemy is close at hand.* I am not paranoid, but I am prepared for the spiritual battle that awaits me as I move into every single day.

It is impossible to read the words of Jesus, examine his life, and miss the fact that our Lord fought spiritual battles. Our Savior could see behind the veil of this world and recognize the presence and power of the enemy. If we are to live like Jesus, we must learn from his example. In chapter 4 of both Matthew and Luke, we see Jesus in fierce hand-to-hand combat with the devil. This is at the start of his public ministry. Then, near the end of his ministry, Jesus warns his followers, "Watch and pray so that you will not fall into temptation. The spirit is willing, but the flesh is weak" (Matt. 26:41). From start to finish, and everywhere in between, Jesus was engaged in the battle, and he stands as the example to his followers through all generations.

Beware of the Two Extremes

As we become more like Jesus and enter into the spiritual battles around us, we should be careful that we do not slip into the two extremes when it comes to the reality of spiritual warfare and the presence of the devil. In his classic book *The Screwtape*

Letters, C. S. Lewis describes two groups of people that the devil is thrilled about.

Lewis calls our attention to the *substitious*—the skeptics. These people are not aware of the existence of a spiritual enemy. They are sure Satan is not real and that the devil only exists in the vivid imagination of children or uneducated and simple people. These confident folks are certain that the spiritual world does not exist and that no one should fear devils or demons.

Satan is thrilled with this outlook, because he can walk right in and have his way with these people. They don't stand guard or prepare for a battle, because they are sure there is no enemy. We need to beware that this kind of hubris does not mark our thinking or outlook.

Lewis also warns us about the *superstitious*. They are sure the devil and demons are behind every bush, every rock, car, and corner. Paranoia sets in as this person lives with a constant fear of the enemy and a certainty that an attack is coming at all times.

Satan loves this attitude, because those who think this way can be paralyzed and made ineffective by their fear. These people are so focused on the presence of the enemy that their eyes are no longer on the risen Savior, their glorious God, and the powerful Holy Spirit. That is why praying with your eyes open to the presence and power of God is essential.

When we are aware of the enemy and prepared for the battle, we are not skeptics. We acknowledge the presence and the work of the enemy. But we are not superstitious. Our focus is not on the enemy but on our Maker and Savior. We are not paralyzed by fear but amazed by grace and empowered by the Spirit for the battles we will face.

Armor and Weapons for the Battle

In Ephesians 6 we see a list of defensive armor we should put on so we can walk in victory as we face spiritual battles. We are to put on the full armor of God, and I would encourage that you do this, in prayer, whenever you feel you are headed into battle.

My suggestion is that you pray,

Lord, I put on the belt of truth, may it be tight against my waist. I put on the breastplate; let your righteousness be mine. Fit my feet with the gospel of peace and make me surefooted for the battle. I hold the shield of faith and ask that I can use it to block and put out every flaming arrow the enemy shoots at me. Cover my head and mind with the helmet of salvation.

One by one, put on the pieces of spiritual armor.

Once you have done this, you have a great defensive plan. But without offensive tactics and weapons, all you can do is protect yourself. God wants to win the victory. For this to happen, we must take up the weapons he gives for the battle. The first weapon is the sword of the Spirit, which is the Word of God (Eph. 6:17). God's Word can be used to fight back and cut down the enemy. If you wonder about this, just read the accounts of Jesus' wilderness battles with the enemy. In Matthew 4 and Luke 4, we see the Savior intensely fighting against the devil. Over and over our Lord quotes from the Word of God in the Old Testament with the declaration, "It is written!" There is no question that the Word of God is a powerful weapon for our spiritual battles.

Prayer is also a weapon. Right after calling us to take up the sword, the apostle Paul writes:

And *pray* in the Spirit on all occasions with all kinds of *prayers* and *requests*. With this in mind, be alert and always keep on *praying* for all the Lord's people. *Pray* also for me, that whenever I speak, words may be given me so that I will fearlessly make known the mystery of the gospel, for which I am an ambassador in chains. *Pray* that I may declare it fearlessly, as I should. (Eph. 6:18–20, emphasis added)

Take note of how many times the word "pray" is used in this short passage. We are called to use the power of prayer as we fight the enemy and enter spiritual battles.

Some scholars think prayer is the seventh piece of warfare equipment. Others see it as an attitude and behavior that is used with all the pieces of armor. I believe it is the latter of these two. Theologian Klyne Snodgrass explains it this way:

Whether prayer is a seventh piece of equipment is debated. Grammar suggests it is not, or else being alert, which is a parallel to praying, would have to be considered a piece of the equipment as well. But the question is irrelevant, for whether it is a piece of the equipment or the demeanor with which the equipment is worn, neither prayer nor being alert is optional for believers. By definition to be Christ's soldier is to pray and keep alert.[1]

The heartbeat of this idea is that we pray as we put on each piece of our spiritual armor. We pray as we wear the armor through every battle. Prayer becomes not only preparation for the battle, but the battle itself, as we walk and live in the power of the Holy Spirit.

All the *All*'s

As we learn to pray with our eyes, ears, and heart open, we will discover the power of prayer for the battle. In Ephesians 6 we are reminded that we can and should be praying at all times. Notice the word "all" and how it is used, over and over, in one simple verse: "And pray in the Spirit on *all* occasions with *all* kinds of prayers and requests. With this in mind, be alert and always keep on praying for *all* the Lord's people" (v. 18, emphasis added).

There is a universal and sweeping sense to warfare prayers. We are praying on all occasions. There are not moments when we drop our guard and act like the battle is over. Every moment provides an opportunity to see the spiritual battles around us and enter in through passionate and faith-filled prayers. We lift up all kinds of prayers with our eyes open physically or figuratively as we live for Jesus. As we give praise and thanks, we battle the enemy and exalt Jesus, the Victor. As we confess sin and ask for power to repent, we see spiritual strongholds broken and God's glory revealed. As we declare the name of Jesus and pray in his authority, the enemy flees and battles are won.

We are also called to pray for all of God's people. That is a massive undertaking. Praying for all of God's people means not only lifting up other believers in our church, our community, and our nation, but in other churches, denominational tribes, and nations. Kevin and I often pray for other believers as we drive past churches. We pray for God's power, presence, blessings, and kingdom to break out in their midst.

If we pray all the *all*'s in this passage, we will find ourselves praying more than ever, and we will see the power of Jesus overcome the work of the enemy in our lives, homes, communities, and world.

Keep the Door Shut . . . Tight!

As we discern where the enemy is at work, we learn to lift up warfare prayers in the flow of an ordinary day. We are not paranoid, but we are always prepared to stand against the enemy.

We are not superstitious, we are not substitious, we are soldiers. This means we are on guard, prepared, and ready to fight.

There is a simple little acronym that is often used in recovery groups to help people be ready to fight against moments of temptation. Since we know who the tempter is, we can use this tool to sharpen our thinking and prepare our hearts for battle. The word is HALT. Each letter represents a word and idea that reminds us about times the enemy is more prone to attack with lies, enticements, and temptations. Our job is to be prepared and ready to fight back.

My husband and I wrote a small group curriculum with Robert Morris, a pastor from Texas who teaches on spiritual warfare. In his book *Truly Free*, he writes about how a person would lock their house up tight if they knew that a burglar was just outside. No one would leave a door slightly open in a situation when they knew someone was planning to rob them. As believers, we have an enemy who is a robber, a liar, a deceiver, and a prowling lion. With this in mind, we should shut and lock every door that might offer a point of entry into our life. Here are four times that we can accidently leave a door open. These four words spell the acronym HALT!

Beware when you are **hungry***.* When you have pushed hard, poured out, and your body is weary with physical hunger, be careful. This is a time when the enemy can come and entice you to fill yourself with something that promises to satisfy. All kinds of temptations can be launched in these moments. This was the tactic the enemy used with Jesus in the wilderness when he had fasted and was hungry (Matt. 4:1–4). When you face physical hunger, fill your body with healthy food and don't fall for the temptation to "satisfy" yourself with things that don't truly satisfy.

*Beware when you are **angry**.* Anger can become a springboard for all kinds of temptations, and the enemy would love to launch you into actions, words, and behaviors that could have lasting negative effects on your life and relationships. The apostle Paul warns us, "'In your anger do not sin': Do not let the sun go down while you are still angry, and do not give the devil a foothold" (Eph. 4:26–27). When we live with unresolved anger and let it poison our life, the enemy gets a foothold. We need to be aware of this and deal with our anger in a godly way.

*Beware when you are **lonely**.* Loneliness in our world is a growing epidemic. Even with all kinds of connections, contact, virtual friends, and group gatherings, we can still find ourselves lonely. We must be aware that times of loneliness can become a place where the enemy can tempt us to fill ourselves with unhealthy relationships, substances, or activities. In these times we should recognize our need for genuine Christian community and the value of being an active part of the body of Christ.

*Beware when you are **tired**.* Fatigue and exhaustion are fertile ground for poor choices. The enemy sees when we are weary and knows our defenses can be down and weak. We need to care for our bodies, get good sleep, and stay fresh. This is a spiritual discipline that will help us in the battle. I love the book *The Good and Beautiful God* by James Bryant Smith. I have used it as a discipleship resource as I have mentored many women. It is the first in a three-book set called The Apprentice Series. The first exercise James offers to help Christians grow in spiritual maturity surprised me. To sum it up, it is about checking our sleep patterns and making sure we are well rested. I thought it would be something lofty like deep study of the Bible or passionate prayer. It was about rest. What a reminder of the importance of watching our personal gauges and being sure we are refreshed.

It Is Not a Fair Fight Anymore!

Gary Thomas, a wonderful pastor and writer, was visiting our church to preach and lead a seminar on the topic of "Sacred Parenting." One of the many things he said that struck me was, "It is not a fair fight anymore." He was talking about how children and young people are exposed to sexual images and content at such an early age through online connections, cable channels, and the staggering availability of pornography. In the past people had to go find this content, purchase it, and keep it hidden. Now, with a swipe and a few clicks, phones, tablets, computers, and TVs become a portal to a world of temptation. The fight has changed and it is not fair.

The truth is, when it comes to spiritual warfare, it has never been fair. Satan has no rules, no boundaries, and no conscience. He delights in the ruin of lives, the destruction of marriages, the collapse of churches, the end of friendships, the demise of families—any devastation he can bring.

The good news is, we follow and serve a God who has power beyond our imagination. He is greater than the enemy of our soul. We follow a God who can prepare a young shepherd boy to bring down a Goliath (1 Sam. 17); our God can empower an Elijah to stand in victory over 850 false prophets (1 Kings 18); as God's people march in obedience, the walls of Jericho fall (Josh. 6); when God is present, the Red Sea parts (Exod. 13–15); in the power of God, the dead rise and sin is conquered (Matt. 28; 1 Cor. 15).

I suppose, when I really think about it, in an ultimate sense, it is *not* a fair fight. God is sovereign. He rules the universe.

Christ has broken the back of Satan. Christ is risen! The Holy Spirit is present in our lives. Our God always wins!

Your Prayer Journey

Commit to lift up a protection prayer for a person you love. Identify where you feel the enemy is attacking and pray against the devil's tactics, in the name of Jesus, every time you think of this person. As you pray, reflect on the Bible passages from this chapter that assure you of the presence of God in your life and the power of God over the enemy. Ask God to show you the places in your life where you have left a door open for the enemy to slip a foot in. As the Holy Spirit reveals these areas, confess them. Pray for the power of God to shut these doors so you can walk in new levels of holiness and obedience.

Twelve

Replace Worry with Prayer

The more you pray, the less you'll panic.
The more you worship, the less you worry.
You'll feel more patient and less pressured.

RICK WARREN

For almost four decades I was a runner. I met God as I ran. I prayed with my eyes open as I ran through spring rainstorms, hot and muggy Michigan summer days, pristine fall days with leaves crunching underfoot, and even freshly fallen snow. I drank in God's beauty and glory with each stride, and God spoke to me in powerful ways.

Then, with heartbreaking abruptness, my running came to an end. Back pain, neck problems, and a spinal surgery put an end to my daily runs. One of the primary activities that connected me to God was no longer an option for me. I still miss it.

In an effort to find a new way to exercise and be outside, I took up swimming. Low impact and less-jarring movement was just what the doctor ordered . . . literally. I went shopping for earplugs, a swim cap, and my first pair of goggles. Since this swimming thing was all new to me, I put on the goggles as tight as I could to assure myself that no water would get in. My goggles actually ended up leaving strange-looking indentations around my eyes for hours after I got out of the pool. Eventually I got the technical issues figured out, loosened my goggles a bit, and stopped disfiguring my face every time I swam.

When I wear my goggles, the water and swimming environment is crystal clear. I can see everything. Occasionally, I forget my goggles. When I do, it is an entirely different experience. I can't open my eyes for very long because of the chlorine. When I do open my eyes, everything is blurry. My depth perception is off. It takes away the fun and becomes a lot less enjoyable.

I have come to look at praying with my eyes open like swimming with a good pair of goggles. When we go through each day ready to pray at any moment, we are more aware of God's presence and power at work. We get more in tune with our environment, knowing how to interact with what is going on around us by praying more. The things that seem out of focus become clearer. In these moments we learn that prayer is not about a specific posture, place, or pattern of words. It is something we can do all through our day, no matter what we are involved in. I believe we get a clearer vision of how God wants us to live with him, like him, and for him.

Prayer and Worry

Because I have good goggles and have learned how to use them, I can swim with my eyes wide open. I pray as I swim. I pray for family members and friends as I do my laps. I lift up prayers for people in our church and in my community who are hurting. I praise and worship the God who loves us with everlasting love.

One morning, I had woken up thinking about a situation in the life of a loved one. I was burdened and worried for this person. I went to the pool to do laps. My goggles were in place, my eyes wide open; I launched into prayer.

After several laps I realized I was still praying for this same concern. First I thought to myself, "Wow, I really spent a lot of time praying for this one concern." Then the Holy Spirit gently spoke this truth into my heart: *You have shifted from prayer to worry.* It was a shocking wake-up call. It was true. It was a hard but important moment in my prayer life.

Prayer and worry are radically different. But sometimes when I think I am praying, I am actually reciting my worries to God rather than giving them to him. When we take our pattern of worry, talk to God about it, and seek to justify our anxiety, we miss the opportunity to actually pray about our worry and find peace. Since I have identified this pattern in myself, I have tried to learn how to move from worry to prayer.

- When I **worry**, I bring my concerns, my fears, and my anxieties to God and recite them before him. Then I keep them for myself and continue on in my worry. When I am engaged in **prayer**, I seek to bring these things to God and leave them at his feet, trusting him to deal with them.

- When I **worry**, I am focused and fixated on the burden or problem I am facing. Authentic **prayer** turns my mind off the anxiety-producing situation and locks my attention on the God who has all power to overcome what I am facing.

- When I **worry**, I stay wound up and anxious. When I lift up genuine **prayers**, I find peace and my heart is calmed because I know God has heard me and he cares.

For everyone who deals with worry and anxiety, this is a better way to live. God offers a path of peace that comes through prayer. To walk this path, we must commit to take a faith-growing journey that will help us replace worry with prayer.

My Journey

During my son Zach's college years, he and his buddy Steve had an opportunity to travel to New Zealand for a month. He was excited to hike some of the amazing trails and terrain of that beautiful country. Zach was thrilled about the adventure, but I can't say I was. I found myself worrying, a lot! I have a mother's heart, and no matter how old my sons are, I will always be, as they affectionately call me, their "Momma."

I have to be honest. I am often tempted to worry instead of pray. I know this is not healthy or helpful, but I seem to be very good at worrying. It comes naturally! With this in mind, I have spent years trying to pray when I find myself anxious or worried about something or someone I love. So when my firstborn son told me he was getting on a plane and traveling to the other side of the planet for a month, I was profoundly aware that I needed some supernatural help to make it through.

I remember waking up on the morning before Zach was to embark on this great adventure. I had never had any of my sons travel so far away and for so long. This was new territory for me. I found myself thinking, *I can't wait until this month is over and Zach is home safe and sound.* As this thought flashed through my mind, I felt a gut-wrenching reality. I was wishing my month away. Before Zach left, I was already worrying about the next thirty days. I knew this was not God's plan for my life.

I asked myself, "Sherry, what kind of faith do you have?"

In this moment I felt a deep conviction that I had to bring my concerns before the Lord. I needed to exchange my worry for prayer. So I prayed about my anxiety. Over the next couple of days that is exactly what I tried to do. I brought my worry to God and tried to place it in his capable and all-powerful hands. Unfortunately, I left my times of prayer carrying the same burdens with me. I did not lay them before God. I did not put my trust in him. I failed to surrender my son to his heavenly Father. I simply spent a lot of time worrying before God. In a sense, my prayers were really a spiritualized form of worry, or what I call "worry prayers." Something needed to change.

As Zach began his trip on the other side of the globe, far from family, hiking and scaling rugged terrain, I began my own climb. The Lord moved me to reflect on and meditate on Philippians 4:4–7.

> Rejoice in the Lord always. I will say it again: Rejoice! Let your gentleness be evident to all. The Lord is near. Do not be anxious about anything, but in every situation, by prayer and petition, with thanksgiving, present your requests to God. And the peace of God, which transcends all understanding, will guard your hearts and your minds in Christ Jesus.

Of course I was familiar with this passage. I knew the basic message, but it did not control my heart and shape my mental outlook. I was praying with my eyes closed to the staggering truth of these Spirit-infused words. I was not praying with my eyes, ears, heart, and life wide open to God's presence, power, and goodness.

I wanted the "peace of God" to fill me. God wanted me to know that he was ready to guard my heart and change my way of thinking. This would be the precursor to me being saturated with peace beyond my understanding.

Thanksgiving

In desperation, I got real honest with God and prayed, "Lord, please help me release my worry and anxiety. Teach me to give my son to you, even when it feels painful and unnatural." As I prayed, the Lord put a specific line on my heart: *Worrying will not help one single bit.* The truth of Philippians 4:4–7 started to come alive in my soul. Worrying would not help, but prayer, trust-filled prayer, would make a difference. From that moment on, every time I started worrying about Zach—and that was quite often at first—I would seek to exchange it for authentic prayer. Worry would not help one single bit, but prayer would. I was ready to look with fresh eyes at this passage about worrying.

I read the passage again and again, seeking to live out all the truth of the Scriptures. Then, like a veil being lifted from my eyes and mind, I read the two words I had seen but not fully understood. One parenthetical thought that had been there in the passage for almost two thousand years. It jumped off the page, captured my heart, and has been changing me ever since. These two words, and my effort to live them out with passion and devotion, have launched me on a continual journey of exchanging worry for prayer.

Here are the two transformational words: "with thanksgiving."

I understood in a fresh, new way why we must be thankful when we pray. Just prior to the clear exhortation in the passage of Philippians 4:6, in verse 5 we are reminded that the Lord is near. You can pray and avoid anxiety because the God of the universe is ready to help you anytime, anywhere. As the psalmist declares in Psalm 120:1, "I call on the LORD in my distress, and he answers me."

We must realize that God is in charge of all things. He rules the world and he can take care of our lives and those we love. This is not a guarantee that everything will go our way. It is not a promise that life will be painless. For me, it was a realization that my world-traveling son actually could end up in harm's way. But my worry would do nothing to help him . . . absolutely nothing! However, God, on the other hand, is not only near but also able to deliver, protect, and help. Faithful and passionate prayer to the God who is near had power to guard and guide him.

I began to add thanksgiving to each of my prayers. I expressed thanks for my son, for his health, and for his friend Steve who is a sensible and Jesus-loving man. I thanked God for Lloyd and Jan, sweet friends who live in New Zealand, who offered to make their home a staging point for Zach and Steve's adventures. I thanked God that Zach was a person who made wise decisions.

With my eyes wide open, through the flow of the remaining thirty days, I thanked God over and over again as I asked him to take care of my son: *Thank you, God, that I can come to you in prayer and trust you. Thank you that Zach and Steve rented a car rather than hiking everywhere. I give you thanks that you are on the throne at all times and in all places . . . even on the other side of the planet.* When worry would sneak in stealthily or come rushing into my heart and mind screaming for my attention, I would pray: *Please watch over Zach and Steve. Thank you that the guys have enough money to make it home. I lift up thanks that Zach has a phone in case of an emergency. Thank you that you rule every inch of this planet!* When doubts and anxiety would try to slip a foot in the door of my life and move back in, I would pray: *Thank you that you love Zach more than I do.*

I kept lifting up prayers of thanks and trust to the God who placed my son in my arms and sent his only Son to save lost and broken people. *Lord, I continue to ask for your care over my son. I thank you that Zach has placed his faith and life in your hands. He is washed clean of all sin. Jesus is his Savior. If Zach does not come home, I know with unbending faith that heaven is his true home.*

Some years after learning this prayer lesson, I had the privilege of writing a small group study with Ann Voskamp based on her book *One Thousand Gifts*. In this book and small group study, Ann calls God's people to relentlessly, joyfully, and creatively make an ongoing list of "One Thousand Gifts" God has given them. This is a call to intentional and persistent thankfulness. I have learned that thankfulness is one of the keys to overcome the power of worry.

Just for full disclosure, I made it through the month and my son Zach came home safely and full of fascinating stories. As the years have passed, I have prayed for Zach many more times, because New Zealand was the first of many more traveling adventures. He had been changed through this first experience and so had I. I realized, in the depth of my soul, that worrying does not help one single bit. Prayer, on the other hand, "with thanksgiving" makes all the difference in the world.

Trust

The question is not, will we face times of stress and worry-producing moments in life? We will. The real question is, will we trust God no matter what we face? Praying with our heart wide open is about understanding that we can trust God in the midst of everything we encounter in this life. The writer of Proverbs puts it this way:

> Trust in the LORD with all your heart
>> and lean not on your own understanding;
> in all your ways submit to him,
>> and he will make your paths straight. (Prov. 3:5–6)

Over and over in the Bible we are assured that the God we worship is trustworthy, in the very core of his being. Isaiah tells us that "he tends his flock like a shepherd: He gathers the lambs in his arms and carries them close to his heart; he gently leads those that have young" (Isa. 40:11). We can trust God as the Good Shepherd of our life and our soul. The psalmist reinforces this when he writes,

> Come, let us bow down in worship,
>> let us kneel before the LORD our Maker;
> for he is our God
>> and we are the people of his pasture,
>> the flock under his care. (Ps. 95:6–7)

We can trust in this God with confident certainty. We don't have to be ruled by anxiety.

In Proverbs we are warned that we should never lean on our own understanding (Prov. 3:5). Worry, in a strange way, is a declaration that we don't trust God, but are leaning on our own strength and ability to navigate hard times. When we worry in front of God and keep our burdens on ourselves, we are acting like we can handle these things better than he can.

Proverbs instructs us to follow the way of wisdom and acknowledge God in all our ways. This means we admit we can't fix our messes, overcome our anxieties, or worry away our worries. Instead, we place our trust in the Lord and give him our burdens.

Trade

In the book of Isaiah we are called to trade a lie for the truth. I encourage you to read this passage (at least twice) very slowly. If you are in a place where you can do so, read it out loud. Ask yourself this question: what or who is being carried? Don't respond too quickly. There is more than one answer.

> Listen to me, you descendants of Jacob,
>> all the remnant of the people of Israel,
> you whom I have upheld since your birth,
>> and have carried since you were born.
> Even to your old age and gray hairs
>> I am he, I am he who will sustain you.
> I have made you and I will carry you;
>> I will sustain you and I will rescue you.
>
> With whom will you compare me or count me equal?
>> To whom will you liken me that we may be
>> compared?
> Some pour out gold from their bags
>> and weigh out silver on the scales;
> they hire a goldsmith to make it into a god,
>> and they bow down and worship it.
> They lift it to their shoulders and carry it;
>> they set it up in its place, and there it stands.
> From that spot it cannot move.
> Even though someone cries out to it, it cannot answer;
>> it cannot save them from their troubles. (Isa. 46:3–7)

There are two contrasting and shocking pictures being painted in this passage. I had read this Scripture many times through the years before it came into focus and struck my heart. The first picture is of a God who carries us.

Look at the passage. Let it touch you deeply and strengthen your trust in the God who loves you. From birth to old age, God carries his beloved people. He has carried you from before you were aware . . . before you could walk. He will carry you when you can no longer move in your own power. The God we worship is powerful and present, even when we don't recognize it. He rescues us and his love for us is incomparable. When we recognize this God as our God, we can lay our burdens and worries at his feet. We can pray to this God with confidence.

In the passage there is also another radically different picture. There are people who make their own god. They take gold and silver and fashion an idol. They try to place trust in this human invention, but it has no breath, no power, no life, and no love. These people lift their false god onto their own shoulders and carry it. Their god becomes a burden they must transport from place to place. They can't really pray to a god like this or trust an idol to protect and deliver them.

Praying with our heart wide open is knowing the God we worship. This God made us and carries us. He can be trusted because he is present and powerful. When we reduce God to a human invention, a mere idol, then we must carry him. When this happens, we do not trust God to deliver, protect, or save us. What he wants is for us to lay down all idols and trade them for the God who promises to carry us, no matter what we face.

The antidote to worrying can be found in living out the exhortation in Philippians 4. When we pray "with thanksgiving," our eyes turn to God and our thinking changes, and that affects our heart. Our eyes are fixed on God in all of his faithfulness and power. When we trust in God and not our own understanding, he guides our path. When we trade powerless idols for the true God who carries us from the womb to the final days of this life, our confidence grows. Worry dies and faith is given new birth!

Your Prayer Journey

Root worry out of your prayer life. Bring an area of your life that tends to cause anxiety before the Lord in prayer. Flood this situation or concern with thanksgiving. Reflect on all you can think of that leads you to be thankful, and let these thoughts rule your heart and prayers. Then, think about the many ways God has been present, powerful, and trustworthy in this area of your life. Every time you feel worry pop up in your heart or your prayers, battle it with declarations of thankfulness and trust.

A simple guide to praying,
using Scripture as your guide when worry is present.

*Bringing My Anything
and Everything to God*

PHILIPPIANS 4:6–7

_____

(your name)

Do not be anxious about anything,

_____

(your anything)

but in everything, by prayer and petition,
with thanksgiving,

_____

(your thanksgiving)

present your requests to God.

_____

_____

(your request)

And the peace of God,
which transcends all understanding,
will guard your hearts and your minds
in Christ Jesus.

PRAYING WITH **LIVES**

WIDE
OPEN

When we pray with our life wide open, we allow the Holy Spirit to transform our behavior, change our direction, and shape our daily decisions. As we do this, opportunities to communicate with God come flooding in with surprising regularity. We no longer "try to pray" or "work at praying more." Speaking to God and hearing from our Lord become the norm.

As our life becomes a dialogue with God, we also find ourselves praying *for* others with consistency and *with* others with growing regularity. The little and inconsequential things become an occasion to talk with God, and the big things move us to conversation with the only one who can manage the universe and our lives.

Praying with our life open to God will lead us to the undeniable conclusion that God hears our prayers, God delights to answer, and something happens every time we pray.

Thirteen

Praying for Others

When I pray for another person, I am praying for God to open my eyes so that I can see that person as God does, and then enter into the stream of love that God already directs toward that person.

PHILIP YANCEY

"I'll be praying for you!" We have all said these words. We mean it when we make this promise. We really do.

Most of us have had times when we make a commitment to pray for another person and then it slips our mind. We are not trying to be thoughtless or uncaring. We are actually completely sincere and serious when we assure another person that we will pray. We mean it. We plan to. We just forget.

We bump into that person at the store or see them at church the next week and realize, "I never prayed." We might even shoot up a quick prayer when we see them, assuring ourselves that we can now tell them we had prayed for them.

If you have been a Christian for any length of time and believe in the power of prayer, you can identify with this scenario in some way. We believe in prayer. We are committed to pray for others. But sometimes we get distracted or forget to pray.

When I am with someone who needs prayer, I am working on being more intentional about praying for him or her in the moment. First, I will often ask, "May I take a moment and pray with you right now?" If they are agreeable, I will pray right there, sometimes with eyes closed and often with eyes wide open. We will think about the privilege and power of praying *with* people in the next chapter.

Second, I often assure people with these words: "I will be praying for you as the Lord brings you to mind." What is so beautiful is that as we grow in our understanding of a posture open to "pray continually," God brings people to our mind and heart at just the right time and more often than we would remember on our own.

The night before I was developing this chapter of the book, God reminded me to pray for someone. I have a dear friend whose relationship is now counted in decades rather than years. She and her husband are going through a long-term and difficult challenge in life that includes physical pain, legal entanglements, and relational challenges. I haven't talked to this friend in months, but last night as I lay in bed trying to fall asleep, this couple was strongly on my heart and mind. I lifted them up in prayer, asking God to strengthen them. I made my request to God with the eyes of my heart wide open to their pain, need, and situation. I cried out to the God who loves them and asked for relief from the burden they have been carrying for a couple of years.

The truth is, it had been some time since they came to my heart. They live two thousand miles away, and I don't get those natural prayer prompters when I "bump into them" because they are so far away. But that night God moved me to pray. After interceding for them, I finally dozed off.

The next morning I woke up to a text from this particular friend. It can be months between us exchanging texts, but the very morning after I prayed for her late at night, she sent me a quick note, not about her situation, but actually she just needed a picture from me taken a few years back. I responded by telling her that God had placed her on my heart the night before and that I had prayed for her. She sent a text right back that started with one simple word: "WOW!" She went on to let me know that they were going into a meeting that very morning that proved to be an important one in this ongoing struggle, and she was so touched by my prayers. I communicated to her that normally I would have just prayed for her and not shared about the prompting, but because she had texted me, I wanted her to be aware of what I felt was a tangible way God was encouraging her and letting her know that he is there for her during this difficult time. She was encouraged and strengthened. I believe God wanted to do that through this prayer for her. Every time we pray for someone, heavenly power is unleashed, God is present, miracles can happen, and we bring a real person into the throne room of God.

When We Pray for Others, We Are Being Faithful to Scripture

All throughout the Bible the people of God have prayed. Confession, praise, thanksgiving, lament, and a host of other kinds of prayer are lifted from the hearts and lips of God's people. All true prayer is directed to God and inspired by the Holy Spirit.

Among all the ways we speak to God and listen for God is a kind of prayer we call intercession. This is prayer lifted up for a person or situation. These prayers for others unleash the power of heaven and move the hand of God. It is not that we are seeking to pressure God to do something he is reluctant about. Instead, intercession is our way of joining with God on what he desires to do for the people in our lives that we care about.

Over and over the Bible calls us to intercede for others in prayer. We are told by the apostle Paul, "Devote yourselves to prayer, being watchful and thankful. And pray for us, too, that God may open a door for our message, so that we may proclaim the mystery of Christ, for which I am in chains" (Col. 4:2–3). James instructs followers of Jesus to "confess your sins to each other and pray for each other so that you may be healed. The prayer of a righteous person is powerful and effective" (James 5:16). Jesus calls us to pray for each other to have the daily bread we need (Matt. 6:11). Again and again the Bible invites and calls us to intercede for each other in prayer.

Intercession is unbounded. It is as great as human need and as wide as the planet we live on. We can pray for effectiveness in sharing faith, for healing, for daily bread, and for every other need we see as we walk through life with our eyes wide open. As you walk down the street, you can notice the needs around you and pray. As you drive around your community and see the brokenness, pray. Every time you intercede for anyone, you are following the call of God's Holy Word.

When We Pray for Others, We Become More like Jesus

Jesus was the great intercessor. In chapter 17 of John's Gospel, we review Jesus' High Priestly Prayer. Jesus was praying for his followers near the end of his life and ministry. The Savior interceded for them. He asked for protection from the enemy and spiritual growth in their lives. This prayer of Jesus should inspire and teach us.

Next, our Savior turned his intercessory prayers to you and me. Jesus lifted up the people who would come to faith through the ministry of the first disciples. He was praying for us! Here is part of Jesus' intercessory prayer: "That all of them may be one, Father, just as you are in me and I am in you. May they also be in us so that the world may believe that you have sent me" (John 17:21). Unity and a common vision are the heart of Jesus, so he prayed for us to experience these realities.

The intercessory ministry of Jesus continues today. In Romans 8 we have this assurance: "Who then is the one who condemns? No one. Christ Jesus who died—more than that, who was raised to life—is at the right hand of God and is also interceding for us" (v. 34). The resurrected Savior is presently praying for us. What a reminder of how we become more like Jesus when we pray for each other! Whenever we lift up an intercessory prayer that is in line with the heart and will of Jesus, we are sharing in the ministry our Lord is engaged in today.

When our three sons were quite young, we had a guest preacher visit our church and bring the Sunday message. His name is Ajith Fernando and he serves the church in his home country of Sri Lanka. While at our church, Ajith stayed in our home and we became close friends in faith immediately. Ajith, his dear wife Nelun, and their family have invested their lives serving the church through leading youth ministry, working with drug addicts, training leaders internationally, and writing some of the most insightful books of our generation. Over the past two decades God has bound our hearts together and made us one. Although we have only spent time together twice, and we have not seen each other face-to-face for almost two decades, we are family.

You might wonder how we could have such fondness for each other and feel so united over the miles and years. The answer is simple—we pray for each other. Hundreds of times over the past twenty years we have exchanged prayer needs and interceded for each other. In doing so, we have become more like Jesus and our hearts have been united, even as Jesus prayed.

When We Pray for Others, We Are Being the Church

A quick survey of the early church in the book of Acts paints a picture of a praying people. In almost every chapter you will find references to praying. They prayed for each other as a normal part of their community life. When there was a need, they lifted it up. This was not an occasional special prayer service; it was the flow of their life as followers of Jesus, the Great Intercessor. When people were sick, they prayed. When a new mission was being started, they prayed. When they needed wisdom, intercession was the normal response. Take time to read the book of Acts and take note of every time the people of God prayed for someone or something. This will propel you forward in your commitment to pray for others.

One morning as I woke up, I found myself thinking of my friend Betsy. I didn't really register it, but she came to my heart and mind a number of times through the day. I have learned that this is often a move of the Holy Spirit leading me to pray. I lifted Betsy up in prayer as I washed the dishes, as I did some other chores, and as I did my church work and my writing ministry. By the end of the day it struck me that I had prayed for my friend several times throughout the day. I sent her a text. I didn't go into the details. I just let her know that God had put her on my heart throughout the day and that I had prayed for her.

Betsy called me and said, "You have no idea how I needed your prayers today." She shared with me that a family member was in the hospital and she had been with them all day—it had clearly been a hard twenty-four hours for my friend. She was so grateful that I had been praying throughout the day. Betsy thanked me and said, "Sherry, it so encourages me to know that God was stirring you to pray and that he was letting me know that he cares." It struck me that we were being the church to each other.

As I thought about how God had showed love to Betsy through my prayers, my mind went to the previous Sunday. I ran into a friend I don't see very often. She caught me and said, "Sherry, something kind of interesting happened this past week. I couldn't get you off my heart and mind so I just kept praying for you." As she spoke those words, I found myself trying to hold back my tears. I told her that it had been a rough week. Knowing God had moved her to intercede for me meant more than she could possibly realize. I felt loved by her, but even more, I knew I was loved by my Father in heaven.

Every follower of Jesus has been filled with the very presence of God. The Holy Spirit dwells in us. He wants to move us to regular, natural, passionate prayer for one another. Be sensitive to God's leading. He will often direct you to pray for somebody. Pray for them and let them know that God inspired you to lift them up through intercession. This is one of the ways God grows us together as one body, the church, and continues to show his love toward us.

When We Pray for Others, We Become a Conduit of God's Power

As we walk with people who are facing situations beyond their means and capacity, we will be moved to pray. When we love people and want the best for them, we quickly recognize that our resources are limited at best and nonexistent in some situations. Pastor and writer Max Lucado puts it this way: "Intercessory prayer . . . acknowledges our inability and God's ability."[1] When we pray, we trust God to do what we could never accomplish.

The good news is that the power of God is beyond our comprehension and it can be unleashed as we intercede on behalf of others. Charles Stanley writes, "Our prayers are the link between God's inexhaustible resources and people's needs. . . . God is the source of power, but we are the instruments He uses to link the two together."[2] We do not pretend to think we have the power to meet all the needs we see, change lives, deliver from temptation, or set people free. But God's immeasurable resources can be unleashed through prayer.

Wes and Claudia serve Daybreak Church, a dynamic congregation in West Michigan. After feeling led to pray for Claudia a number of times over a few days, I checked in with her to see how she was doing. I simply let her know that the Lord had been bringing her to my heart and I had just been praying for her. I didn't really say much more. When Claudia realized that my heart was heavy for her, she later shared with me, she had a sense that the Holy Spirit was moving her to be more diligent to check up on some physical concerns she was having about herself, and she felt the nudge from my prayers. When she went to the doctor, she asked them to do a thorough checkup. What followed was that they discovered that she had cancer and needed surgery.

Over the coming weeks, hundreds of people all over the world were interceding for Claudia and her family. God showed up in many ways. The family experienced the strength and comfort of the Holy Spirit. Claudia had the cancer removed and the doctors were amazed that it was localized and isolated.

Claudia and Wes wrote a letter to the many people who had been praying and assured us that they were confident God had done a miracle. The prayers of God's people unleashed the power of heaven. When we pray, bodies can be healed, marriages can be restored, fractured friendships can be made whole, hearts can be opened to Jesus, hope can be restored, and countless other miracles can happen. There is more power in prayer than we can envision in our wildest imaginations.

When We Pray for Others, We Are Moved to Action

Prayer is not passive. It is one of the most active things we will ever do. Not only does prayer unleash the power of heaven, it moves us. When we intercede in concert with the heart of God, we see the hand of God move and things happen. That same God will often call us to enter into his ministry in the world. I can't begin to remember or list all the times I have been praying and have heard the gentle voice of the Spirit call me to do something.

All through the day God stirred me to pray for a wonderful young woman who is married to one of the pastors at our church. By the end of the day I felt I needed to call her and make myself available to serve in some way. My prayers called me to action. It just so happened that she was in the middle of a very busy time and she said it would be so helpful if I could come over and help her with her kids for an afternoon. As we pray in line with God's heart, we should be ready to move into God-inspired action. This is a privilege. It is the way of the Christian.

When We Pray for Others, Our Spiritual Life Is Expanded

On a ministry trip in New Zealand, Kevin and I were doing some training with church leaders. One of the people in the meeting was a convert from another world religion, and he had been distanced from many in his own family for almost three decades. We challenged all those present to intercede, to pray, to seek ways to share their faith organically with the people God had placed in their life. We encouraged them to be creative in their prayer life for others, even considering using emails and text messages. We had no idea how this simple exhortation would expand the spiritual life of this one man.

A couple of days later, at another training time, he came up to Kevin and me. With sadness in his eyes, he explained that he had tried to find a way to break into spiritual conversation with family members for over thirty years and he hit roadblocks at every turn. I could feel his pain. Then his eyes brightened and he explained with joy that he had his first breakthrough.

After our last training time, he shared that the Holy Spirit put on his heart that he should text a short prayer to one of his relatives who was going through a hard time. He followed this prompting and sent her a prayer. She responded with the words, "Thank You," and then a very sweet text message.

This might not seem like a big deal to you or me, but for this man, after what felt like a lifetime of seeking to reach his family, it was the first positive step forward. She was open to his prayer and appreciative. God unleashed power and his presence, and a door was opened to a spiritual conversation. Maybe one day this would lead to a conversation about God's sacrificial love for her. For this man, his whole spiritual life opened up and blossomed when he entered into intercessory prayer in a new way.

When We Pray for Others, the Gospel Spreads

Every conversion is born of a work of the Holy Spirit and the prayers of God's people. If you could track your spiritual legacy back through the heavenly realms, you would see the prayers of God's people are part of your story. For me, it was my parents and grandparents. Their prayers covered me from my mother's womb. For Kevin, it was the prayers of his Granny. It was also the relentless prayers of his sister Gretchen who became a follower of Jesus a year before Kevin. In your story, there have been praying people who partnered with God on your journey to Jesus.

Our prayers can be God's way of sharing grace with other believers and the gospel of God's love with those who are still searching spiritually.

Prayer Reminders

As we pray for others, there are a number of important reminders the Bible gives us. These are some of the things we can miss if we are not attentive and sensitive to God's direction as we pray. Here are five things I find helpful to remember. Each of these helps me keep my prayer life on track.

1. *Pray for people in places of authority.* God has put people in places of authority and we are called to pray for them. Governmental leaders, law enforcement personnel, civic servants, and others in roles of influence should be covered with the prayers of God's people (1 Tim. 2:2). We can ask for wisdom and protection, for God's hand on their life and family, and for the presence of Jesus to be revealed to them. We don't have to agree with someone to pray for them. Our prayers cross all boundaries to bring God into all situations.

2. *Cry out to God for those who are far from Jesus.* Our Savior called us to pray to the God of the harvest and ask him to send us out with the message and love of Jesus (Matt. 9:35–38). In the book of Acts, the prayers of God's people preceded the revival of Pentecost (chaps. 1–2). It is natural for most of us to pray for other believers. We should also be praying with fervor and consistency for the people in our life who have not yet discovered that God loves them and that Jesus' sacrifice is enough to wash them clean of sin and begin a new life.

3. *Intercede for all of God's people.* We not only pray for the Christians close to us but for all of God's people (Eph. 6:18). Many churches pray for needs in their congregation. At Shoreline Community Church, where my husband and I serve on staff, we have a weekly practice. We pray for other local congregations. We actually call the other Christian churches and ask, "What can we pray for you in our weekend services?" Each Sunday, as a congregation, we pray for one church in our community, for their lead pastor by name, and for specific needs and challenges they are facing. We are part of one body of Christ and believe praying for each other (as churches) is very important.

4. *Lift up the people who see themselves as your enemy.* Jesus called us to pray, even for those who treat us badly and persecute us (Matt. 5:44). If you know what the early church would face under Roman persecution in the coming years, this exhortation would shock you. If first-century Christians could pray for those who were ravaging the church, destroying Christian communities, and martyring fellow believers, we can certainly pray for those who are hostile to us and our faith.

5. *Pray for God's will to be done.* When Jesus taught his followers how to pray, he told us to pray for his kingdom, not our own personal empires, to come. He directed us to pray, not for the fulfillment of our personal whims, but for his will to be done (Matt. 6:10). In all of our prayers for ourselves, for Christian friends, for nonbelievers, for governing authorities, and even for enemies, we are to pray for God's will to be done.

If we can pray in God's will, then we can pray in the name of Jesus. When we pray in the name of Jesus, we can have confidence that God will hear and answer our prayers.

Your Prayer Journey

In the coming month, try doing a 1-1-1 Prayer. This is something Lee Strobel taught at the Organic Outreach Conference we hold at Shoreline Church. The idea is simple. You pray for a person who is not yet a follower of Jesus. Commit to intercede for them and ask God to soften their heart, open them to the love of Jesus, and give opportunities for Christians (including you) to share the gospel of Jesus. Here is the 1-1-1 part: What you commit to do is set an alarm and reminder on your phone or watch for 1:00 p.m. every day. At this time, pray for this one person for one minute. That's it. Of course, if 1:00 p.m. is not the best time, you can adjust this. This is one way to remind ourselves to live a life open to "pray continually."

Fourteen

Praying with Others

If we truly love people, we will desire for them far more than it is within our power to give them, and that will lead us to prayer.

RICHARD FOSTER

It was my sophomore year at Calvin College and I was terrified. I had been hired as a resident assistant for the young women on my floor. At the first leaders' meeting they told me I had to do something that made me question whether or not I could be an RA. I did not know how I was going to do it. I went through moments of feeling nervous, anxious, and genuinely afraid.

You might be wondering, what could the leaders of this Christian college have asked me to do that would paralyze me like this? What strange task had they requested of me? What mammoth expectation could they have heaped on me that would cause this level of concern? The answer is simple; they asked me to pray out loud with the girls on my floor.

I had grown up with praying parents, I was part of a praying church, I had been a person of prayer from my youngest days and memories. But praying out loud with others, aside from my parents, scared me more than I could put into words.

I finally talked with my roommate, Connie, the other resident assistant for our floor, and told her about how I felt. I confessed my fear and the temptation to find some way out of this dilemma. Her response was as beautiful and sweet as her heart: "Sherry, why don't we just pray together every morning. You can practice with me. There won't be any pressure, we will just talk to God our Father together." For some reason, this felt safe and I agreed. Morning after morning we prayed. We spoke to Jesus as a friend. We lifted up reverent prayers to the God who rules the universe. We thanked God for his blessings and praised him for his goodness.

Before I knew it, I had grown comfortable praying out loud with my friend. I still had a little nervousness, but most of it was gone. When the floor meeting happened and I had to lead in prayer, I was able to do it. I must be honest, it was still a learning curve, but my comfort level grew stronger with time. There were little bouts with fear, but God gave me courage. As the semester went on, praying with the young women on my floor became quite natural.

I learned that praying with others could become a natural part of our life, even when we start out being anxious about it. Since that time in college, praying with others has become more and more a part of my life. I have tried to help people learn to pray in community so they, too, can experience the joy, delight, and power of praying with others.

Jesus Prayed with People

Jesus was a beautiful example of living in a state of perpetual prayer. He certainly modeled the discipline of slipping away to private places for one-on-one times of communication with the Father (Mark 1:35). He also made a point of praying with others. In key times of his ministry Jesus would sometimes gather a small cluster of friends (often Peter, James, and John) and slip away for prayer. One time, before Jesus was transfigured, he asked these three friends to go away to the mountain and pray with him (Luke 9:28). It was in this time of prayer retreat with close brothers that the Father declared, "This is my Son, whom I have chosen; listen to him" (v. 35). Jesus loved to talk with the Father in community with others.

When Jesus taught his followers to pray, he called them to do this in community. Have you ever noticed that the Lord's Prayer is a call to seek the face of God with other believers? In this well-known prayer, Jesus did not call us to pray "me and my." Instead, he taught his people to pray, "Our, us, and we!" Read this prayer out loud and emphasize the words in bold italics:

This, then, is how you should pray:

> "*Our* Father in heaven,
> hallowed be your name,
> your kingdom come,
> your will be done,
>   on earth as it is in heaven.
> Give *us* today *our* daily bread.
> And forgive *us* our debts,
>   as *we* also have forgiven *our* debtors.
> And lead *us* not into temptation,
>   but deliver *us* from the evil one." (Matt. 6:9–13,
>   emphasis added)

This does not mean that we shouldn't pray, "My Father in heaven." But it is clear that Jesus is teaching that praying with other believers in Christian community should be commonplace in our lives.

Prayer with Others Should Be Common

Many followers of Jesus feel like I did when I found out that I had to pray out loud with other people. This can cause fear, even for very committed and mature Christians. It can seem strange and out of place for those who have not done it. This anxiety over praying with others can keep people from joining a small group, from accepting a leadership role in the church, and from growing close Christian friendships. I have met wonderful Christians through the years who live with a very real fear about praying in a group or one-on-one with other believers.

God's desire for you is to have rich and meaningful times of prayer one-on-one with him. He also delights when you pray with others in groups, and face-to-face with other Christians. If this comes naturally for you, wonderful! If this makes you nervous, you are in good company. Lots of us have had to grow, learn, and press through our fear until this became a common part of our life. I encourage you to find one person who you respect and trust as a brother or sister in Christ, like I did with my friend Connie, and practice praying out loud with another person. Make this a normal part of your life until you are ready to pray with other people.

I am so thankful that I pressed past my fears. Praying with others has become a rich and meaningful part of many of my relationships. At the end of a phone call I will sometimes pray with whomever I am talking with. After church services, people come to talk with me and I can end up praying with many of them. After they share a need or joy, I simply say, "Can we take a moment and pray together?" These times of prayer are sweet

and filled with the presence of Jesus. They deepen our relationship. When I walk with friends in the hills near our home or at
the beach, we often spend some of the time praying as we walk,
with our eyes wide open. We move in and out of conversation
with each other and conversation with God. It is not unusual
to pray at different points in a one-hour walk with a friend or
with my husband.

Prayer should become part of our connection with God and
with the people in our lives. If we are learning to pray without
ceasing, continually talking with God, we will find ourselves
praying with others. Since much of our life is in community
with people, the only way we can pray continually is to pray
with others.

When prayer becomes part of the fabric of our relationship
with family members, friends, neighbors, and the other people
in our life, we begin to encounter God in our relationships.
Prayer is not just hidden away at home or reserved for bedtime
or pre-meal blessing. It is engrafted in all we do. As we pray,
God shows up; we encounter his presence, power, and glory
in our relationships. The great Christian thinker A. W. Tozer
wrote, "True Christian experience must always include a genuine
encounter with God. Without this, religion is but a shadow, a
reflection, a cheap copy of the original once enjoyed by someone else of whom we have heard."[1] There is no better way to
encounter God in our relational world than to pray together.

Ideas as You Pray with Others

There is not a formula for how to pray. Jesus was clear that
many of the people of his day had fallen into a practice of heap-
ing up words and prayers that had become vacant and empty
(Matt. 6:7). He called his people to pray from their hearts, in

community, and to focus on big themes that should guide our prayer life (Matt. 6:9–13). But our Savior did not give an exact script for prayer. What he gave was a guideline to help us identify key themes and topics that should be lifted up regularly in our prayer life.

With this in mind, we should beware of formulaic prayers and rigid structures. At the same time, there are a number of biblical and practical ideas that will help us move forward in how we pray with others. Here are some of the lessons I have learned along the way.

Ask God to lead you by his Holy Spirit. Prayer should be a natural, normal part of our life. It should also be supernatural. We should be led by the Holy Spirit of God in all we do. Ask God to help you notice good times to pray with others. Invite the Spirit to give you boldness and confidence to say, "Can we take a moment and pray about that?" Look for God-given moments that are natural for praying together.

I have found two very common opportunities to pray with others. One is when we are talking about a hurt, struggle, loss, or place of pain. Stopping to pray at these times should be a reflexive response for followers of Jesus who know that the comfort and strength we need comes from our heavenly Father. There are also times of intense joy, victory, and celebration as we walk through life. In these moments we should be open to say to others, "Can we pause and thank God?" When we have experienced God's goodness, presence, protection, provision, and whatever other good things God is doing, thanks and praise should follow with reflexive regularity.

Pray out of the depths of your relationships. Since prayer comes out of who we are, our prayers with others should reflect the depth and nuance of that relationship. When we have a close and intimate friendship or connection with a family member, our prayers will reflect this relationship and can go deep quickly. When we are first getting to know someone, our prayer with them might be less intense and vulnerable since the relationship is young. This is fine . . . it is to be expected. One of the wonderful benefits of praying with others is that it deepens our relationship as God grows our hearts together as his children.

Be sensitive to the setting and the time. I find there are times when praying together out loud, with eyes closed or open, does not feel appropriate. This is not a matter of being ashamed or embarrassed. It is about wisdom. I have had servers at restaurants we often patronize share an honest pain or struggle and have wanted to pray for them, but felt led by the Spirit to simply say, "I want you to know that I will be praying for you today about your situation." Having them stop in the middle of their work does not seem like the natural or right thing to do.

Some settings lend themselves to praying with eyes wide open more than closed. If I am going to have a time of prayer with someone in a public setting, I sometimes say, "Let's pray with our eyes open." I was meeting with a couple of friends at a coffee shop. It was one of those coffee shops that had long tables that place others very close to you. One of my friends was talking about the future and life-direction she felt God might be taking her. It was a very important moment and seemed like a great time to pray. I spent a few minutes sharing about praying with our eyes wide open and then invited them to pray. To any casual observer, they would have thought we were just talking. To God, it was clear we were praying. We simply invited the Lord of glory into the conversation and kept talking.

As often happens the first time I pray with eyes open with a friend, there was a little awkwardness. But it soon felt very natural. We prayed for the Lord's leading, for wisdom, for clear direction. After we finished praying, both of my friends shared how good it felt to remember that God is with us and to pray in this new, old way of communicating with God.

Pray with people who are not yet followers of Jesus. It surprises people to hear this, but my husband and I pray with our eyes open with nonbelievers. When the opportunity presents itself, we find this very meaningful and rich.

We had just landed in Kansas City and were standing at the baggage claim area. A gentleman came up to my husband and asked if this was the place to pick up luggage for our flight. He said, "Yes," and they began to chat. Kevin asked him, "Are you coming home or leaving home?" He responded, "Kind of both." He went on to explain that he had grown up in the Kansas City area but now his home was on the West Coast. So coming to Kansas City always felt like coming home, even though he had a new home.

Kevin asked, "What brings you back to this area?" The gentleman got very serious and reflective as he said, "I just found out that my mom has stage 4 cancer." He and Kevin talked for a few minutes and two things became clear: this man was deeply in need of prayer and was a spiritual seeker. After hearing some of his story, Kevin asked, "Would you mind if I said a quick prayer for you and your mom as you go to visit with her?" It seemed totally natural and appropriate. The man seemed very touched and said, "I would love that."

Kevin explained that they did not need to bow their heads or close their eyes. He said, "I will lift up a prayer and you can just agree in your heart." After Kevin prayed, they went back to talking. Kevin was able to encourage him and learn more about his story. Before we parted ways, this gentleman asked Kevin,

"Are you a pastor or something?" Kevin said, "Actually, I am, but I would have prayed for you even if I was not."

Over the last decade both Kevin and I have prayed with non-believers more times than we can count. When we offer to pray, with eyes open or closed, they almost always say yes. Every time we pray, God shows up in a special way.

Don't force prayer. It is wonderful to offer prayer. It is a joy when people say yes. It is inappropriate to force the issue. So, if someone is open to pray with you, wonderful. Pray. If someone is not ready, be gracious and patient. Let them know that you are always available to pray with them, but assure them that you will never force the issue.

Rejoice in the great work you see God do, and share each other's burdens. Kevin and I were driving from Auckland to Lake Taupo in New Zealand. We were speaking at a conference for pastors and church leaders from all over the country. The couple driving us, Harataki and Shona, were gracious and kind. We had met them on our two previous trips to New Zealand and had grown very fond of them but did not know them well. Now we had about four hours to really get to know each other.

As we began to share about our lives with one another, I expressed a concern I had in my life. Harataki continued on the conversation by just breaking into prayer, eyes wide open: he was driving. Shona contributed to this conversation with God as well. Of course, I was smiling in the backseat because of this book I was writing at the time, but I was also encouraged because I realized the depth of care they were giving me. They were asking God to move in power in my life. As we drove, they shared some of the joys and challenges they were facing in life, family, and ministry. They have a powerful passion for the people they seek to minister to, and as we drove, we continued on in our prayer time for their ministry concerns. Over the next four hours we must have prayed half a dozen times. We did not say, "Let's pray," or "Shall we stop to pray about that?" Prayer flowed in the course of our conversation. The bond between us grew in this four-hour drive and prayer time. God was weaving our hearts together as we prayed together; lives wide open, eyes wide open.

This drive was a powerful picture of sharing burdens as well as rejoicing together. Prayer is a natural way to express our hearts to God and to support each other. My hope and prayer for you is that regular and natural prayers will flow when you are with other people who know and love Jesus.

Praying with Groups of People

There are unique dynamics when a group of people prays together. This is a different experience than praying one-on-one with another person. Here are some things to be sensitive to when praying in a group.

Pray from your heart. Authentic prayer comes from the depth of our soul. Don't be afraid to let your heart show through when you pray. God knows what is happening inside of you. Be honest in prayer, even when you are with others.

Keep your prayers brief. When you are praying with a group of people, it is always best to be brief with your prayers. You can pray numerous times, but if you go on for an extended time, others might feel they are not welcome to jump in and add their voice. Shorter prayers make room for many to lift their heart before the Lord and for all those gathered to agree with an "Amen!"

Listen and engage. Don't spend your time planning your next prayer. Instead, you should listen to the prayers of others and engage your heart. Agree with them. Pray silently as others are praying out loud. Then, jump in and add your prayer.

Build on the prayers of others. If a person has lifted up a prayer that connects with your heart, agree with their prayer and then build on it. You can pray, "Lord, I agree with Diane and her prayer for strength as she faces this time of loneliness and fear. I ask for your Holy Spirit to descend on her and grant her courage and a deep sense of your presence. Help her know she is never alone." When you listen well, you can be moved to pray in concert with others.

Use normal language. Be careful not to use overly "spiritual" or "churchy" language. When you are praying in a group, it is helpful to use ordinary language so others do not feel they have to mimic and copy super-spiritual-sounding prayers. Work to use conversational language that others can understand. No one should need a theological dictionary just to understand your prayer.

Confidentiality is essential. As you grow in praying in groups, know that some prayers will be surprisingly transparent and even vulnerable. It should be understood that whatever you pray about is private—between God and whoever is in your group. If prayers become fodder for gossip, this will cause people to shut down when they pray with you. Keep people's prayers in confidence and God will draw more people to pray with you.

It is an honor to come into the presence of the Living God. It is a greater honor to know we can talk with him in prayer and that he hears us. This blessing is multiplied when we pray with others. Seek to make this a normal part of your daily life and see how God grows your faith in him and intimacy with the people he has placed in your life.

Your Prayer Journey

Identify a Christian friend or family member that you have never prayed with. Sometime in the coming week, look for an opportunity to pray with this person. When they share a joy or sorrow, ask them if you could pray with them about that together. If it seems appropriate, you might even want to teach them what you are learning about praying with your eyes wide open. A second challenge is to look for an opportunity to pray with someone who is not a Christian. If the door is open and you ask someone if you could pray with them, be sure you let them know that you will be doing the praying (out loud) and they can quietly agree in their heart. If you see this person regularly, be sure to follow up and ask them if they have experienced some kind of answer to the prayer you lifted up together.

Fifteen

Praying for the Little and Big Things of Life

We tend to use prayer as a last resort, but God wants it to be our first line of defense. We pray when there's nothing else we can do, but God wants us to pray before we do anything at all.

OSWALD CHAMBERS

Most of us have had the privilege of meeting a person who is so natural in their life of prayer that they get dubbed a "prayer warrior." I heard this term occasionally as a girl growing up in and around the church. Of course, these people don't have a name tag that says "Prayer Warrior," and they are not given badges or medals to wear on a uniform. They are ordinary people who have deep faith in Jesus and are convicted that the power of God is unleashed through prayer. With this confidence, they pray often, talk to God with passion, and see wonderful answers to prayer.

I met such a person when God brought Alma into my life. What struck me about this humble woman was that she seemed to pray naturally about everything. It did not matter how big or small it was. Alma prayed.

I first encountered Alma when Kevin and I accepted an invitation to speak for a church leaders' conference. The Christian Reformed Church of Australia held a national event for pastors, church leaders, and spouses every two years. This particular year they based their conference on my husband's book *Leadership from the Inside Out*.

Alma was one of the leaders at this conference, and during one of the many sessions Kevin and I led on this topic about the inner life of a Christian leader, she felt a nudge in her heart to begin lifting up a very specific prayer. Her prayer was that someday, if she had the opportunity, she would invite me to be the speaker for their denominational biennial women's gathering. In her heart, this was a big prayer. Would she have influence to help make this happen? Would I be available? Could they afford to bring someone from the other side of the planet over for this event? There were lots of questions and many possible obstacles, but Alma prayed and carried it to the Lord.

About four years later, Alma's opportunity to help find a speaker came. She contacted me. Alma shared all about the women's conference and asked me to pray with her to seek the Lord's direction about me coming to teach at this four-day event. As we prayed, I felt a clear prompting from the Holy Spirit that I was to join the team she was leading to minister to this national gathering of women.

Over the following several months, Alma and I talked over the phone and planned regularly. We prayed every time we communicated. We prayed for the conference and then Alma would pray for my family members by name. I loved how she wove prayer into the natural flow of her life and ministry.

When I arrived in Adelaide, Australia, it was Alma who met me at the airport and hosted me. Our hearts had already been bound together in ministry partnership and through our times of praying together. In the coming days we became sisters. I already knew Alma prayed about the big things. Now I would discover how passionately and effectively she prayed about little things.

Koala Prayers

Early on in our time together Alma told me that she really hoped and prayed that the time at her house before the conference would refresh me. She told me later, it was not only her prayer that I would be refreshed, but that I would get a chance to see a koala while I was there. These shy creatures sleep a lot and often in the daytime. There are actually people who live in Australia and have never seen one outside a zoo. Alma really wanted me to see a koala.

It might seem like a small and even silly prayer to some people. But Alma wanted me to have a sweet experience while in Australia, and she thought it would be nice for me to see some Australian wildlife. Alma believes God cares about the big things and also the smallest of things, so she prays for everything.

My first day in Adelaide, Alma took me on a two-hour walk in a beautiful park. After walking and talking for a bit, Alma said, "I apologize that I keep looking up as we walk, but I am looking for a koala. I would love for you to see one." She was matching her prayer with effort. I told her that I actually had not noticed, but was touched that she was going to great lengths to help me see a koala while I was there. We finished the walk without a sign of one.

As we drove to the retreat center, we went through the eastern suburbs on the way to Belair, where we would have the conference. As we paused at an intersection in one of these suburbs, I got a tickle in my throat. I started coughing and could not stop. Alma said, "That's strange, I wonder if there is something in the air." As she looked up into the trees, to see if that might be the cause of my throat irritation, she smiled and said, "Sherry, look up, there is a koala in that tree." Sure enough, even though we had spent two hours in a park looking for a koala, God surprised us with one in a very strange place.

As we drove on, we laughed and delighted in how God drew our attention to see a koala through a tickle in my throat. In that moment, I experienced a sweet touch of God's love as I realized he had provided a koala for me to see in a surprising and fun way. Through praying for big things, God led me to Australia to teach his Word. Through praying for small things, I got to see a koala and have a special moment with a dear sister in Christ.

A Psalm for Big and Small Things

I love the book of Psalms. This prayer book of God's people leads us to speak with God about the simple delights of life and through the valley of the shadow of death. All through the psalms we learn that both big and small prayers matter to God. In Psalm 103 we see this truth in a vivid way. Read this psalm and reflect on what it might lead you to pray about:

> Praise the LORD, my soul;
>   all my inmost being, praise his holy name.
> Praise the LORD, my soul,
>   and forget not all his benefits—
> who forgives all your sins
>   and heals all your diseases,

who redeems your life from the pit
   and crowns you with love and compassion,
who satisfies your desires with good things
   so that your youth is renewed like the eagle's. . . .

For as high as the heavens are above the earth,
   so great is his love for those who fear him;
as far as the east is from the west,
   so far has he removed our transgressions from us.

As a father has compassion on his children,
   so the LORD has compassion on those who fear
   him;
for he knows how we are formed,
   he remembers that we are dust. (vv. 1–5, 11–14)

God knows us. He is our ever-present and powerful provider. This psalm teaches us to be sure we don't forget "all his benefits."

What benefits has God given you? They are countless and range from the delight of a sparrow landing on a windowsill to the sacrifice of his only beloved Son. God's benefits are small and big.

Our God satisfies us. Each breath of air is his gift. The provision of a job. Good friends. A great meal. A sunny day. God satisfies us with small and big things. Our prayers should reflect the God who meets our needs, gives us benefits, heals our hurts, and forgives our sins.

I love how the Apostles' Creed reminds us that God is intimate and present. It also declares that our God is sovereign and Ruler of the universe. This creed begins like this: "I believe in God the Father Almighty, maker of heaven and earth." God is our Father. He cares about the smallest and most intimate of needs and concerns. God is also almighty. He has the power to do something about the situations we face. We pray to the

God who is both Father and Almighty. Personally, I like that "Father" comes before "Almighty" in this creed.

If you are a parent, you know that you always want your children to come to you with whatever is on their heart, no matter how big or small. How sad it would be for a loving parent to find out that their child had suffered because they failed to come and ask for help. In the same way, God wants his children to approach him with confidence and faith. Our part is to ask. God's part is to decide how to answer our prayer in his sovereign wisdom.

Too Little or Too Much?

Some years ago, when our sons were young, a dear friend came to preach at our church. His name is Ben Patterson and he is a man of prayer who, along with his wife, Lauretta, has had a powerful impact on both Kevin and me. While Ben was preaching, he looked at the congregation and said, "Do we ask too much of God, or too little?"

One of my boys leaned over and said, "Too much!"

Ben went on to say that he believed we do not ask enough of God. He quoted from *The Weight of Glory*, where C. S. Lewis wrote,

> It would seem that our Lord finds our desires not too strong, but too weak. We are half-hearted creatures, fooling about with drink and sex and ambition when infinite joy is offered us, like an ignorant child who wants to go on making mud pies in a slum because he cannot imagine what is meant by the offer of a holiday at the sea. We are far too easily pleased.[1]

Ben went on to explain that Lewis believed we ask too little of God. I would agree.

Though many of us, like my son, might think we ask too much, the truth is that most of us should ask more of the Creator and Sustainer of the universe. He cares about our deepest dreams, pain, fears, and longings. He also cares about the smallest details of our life. The God who made the heavens and the earth also knows the number of hairs on our head and when a sparrow falls from the sky. He cares about all of our life and wants us to bring everything to him in prayer.

Open Wide Your Mouth

I often begin a conference or a longer speaking engagement with a simple picture from Psalm 81:10. The psalmist writes:

> I am the LORD your God,
>   who brought you up out of Egypt.
> Open wide your mouth and I will fill it.

The words that have caught my attention and given me a vivid picture of prayer are "Open wide your mouth." This passage sends the message that God is ready to fill us. The real question is, will we open our mouth, our heart, and our life to receive all he is ready to give?

At conferences I will often invite someone who loves M&Ms to come forward and join me up front. I explain to them that I would love to give them some M&Ms and ask them to prepare to receive the M&Ms I want to give. I have a large bag with me, more than their two hands can hold.

Each time the person will cup their hands together, turn them upward, and seek to make as much space as they can for maximum M&M receiving. I begin pouring M&Ms into their hands . . . as much as they can hold. I remind those listening that

I will give this person as much as they can handle, and I do. I fill their hands until they can't hold one more M&M.

This picture communicates the message. God wants us to open our mouth, our hands, our heart, and our life to receive more. This is not about self-serving childish requests. It is about a God who wants to give us so many benefits that we will never forget how good he is. It is about a heavenly Father who truly is almighty and has more to pour into us than we can possibly handle. Our part is to open wide so God can fill us. Prayer is one of the best ways to open up and receive from God.

Ask more of God. Expect more of God. Seek him for the biggest of things and the "impossible" things. And ask him for the little stuff—he really does care about the smallest details of your life.

At one event where I was speaking, I read Psalm 81:10 as I started. I invited a woman forward to receive as many M&Ms as she could handle. I wanted these loved children of God to get the message and open their mouths wide to receive from the Lord. When I lifted up the jumbo pack of M&Ms and told her to take a posture of receiving, she did *not* open her hands. She did *not* turn them upward. She surprised me and everyone gathered. As the crowd looked on, she did something no one had ever done before. This woman was wearing a long T-shirt and she grabbed the edges of her shirt and carefully turned it into a bowl for her M&Ms.

I smiled and poured. The crowd cheered and laughed. She walked away with *all* of my M&Ms.

We all got the message!

How Little Is Too Little?

As we learn to ask more of God, we will discover that praying with our eyes wide open all through our day will lead us to pray about many things that seem small and even inconsequential. When someone races up behind us while we are driving and follows way too close, we can pray for them and let them pass rather than getting upset and reciprocating with road frustration. When we find ourselves in a situation that seems to be beyond our wisdom, we will reflexively ask for heavenly insight. When a situation seems tense, we pray for the peace of the Holy Spirit. Nothing is too small or mundane to bring before the Lord.

There is a wonderful story I heard years ago about a little boy praying for ice cream. I am not sure of the original source, but the message is memorable and the story worth retelling:

Last week, I took my children to a restaurant. My six-year-old son asked if he could say grace. As we bowed our heads he said, "God is good. God is great. Thank you for the food, and I would even thank you more if Mom gets us ice cream for dessert. And liberty and justice for all! Amen!"

Along with the laughter from the other customers nearby, I heard a woman remark, "That's what's wrong with this country. Kids today don't even know how to pray. Asking God for ice cream! Why, I never!"

Hearing this, my son burst into tears and asked me, "Did I do it wrong? Is God mad at me?" As I held him and assured him that he had done a terrific job and God was certainly not mad at him, an elderly gentleman approached the table. He winked at my son and said, "I happen to know that God thought that was a great prayer."

"Really?" my son asked.

"Cross my heart," the man replied. Then in a theatrical whisper, he added (indicating the woman whose remark had started this whole thing), "Too bad she never asked God for ice cream. A little ice cream is good for the soul sometimes."

Naturally, I bought my kids ice cream at the end of the meal. My son stared at his for a moment and then did something I will remember the rest of my life.

He picked up his sundae and without a word, walked over and placed it in front of the woman. With a big smile he told her, "Here, this is for you. Ice cream is good for the soul sometimes; and my soul is good already."[2]

The point is not that we need to pray for ice cream. The truth is, we can pray about everything, including ice cream.

A Fresh Perspective at Six in the Morning

My sister Dawn walked out of the house early one morning to water her flowers before the heat of the day set in. As she was finishing her task, she tried to open the front door to go back into her house when she realized she had mistakenly locked herself out. Frustrated for a moment, but then in a glimmer of hope, she heard her husband pulling out of the driveway and turning around the corner to head to work. She tried to wave him down, but unfortunately, he thought she was waving goodbye for the day. Frustrated at herself and now at her husband, standing in her pajamas in front of her house, she realized this was not a good start to the day.

After checking all the doors and realizing she really was locked out, she looked at her watch again. Her neighbor had a backup key, but she did not want to knock on her door before 7:00 a.m. She shared with me later, it was at that moment the Holy Spirit reminded her of things we had been talking about—that she can pray continually about anything at any time. So she began to pray.

Over the next hour my sister Dawn met with Jesus. She first asked God to help her deal with the frustration of this experience, owning up to her mistake and realizing that her frustration toward her husband proved to be a little comical. As she sat enjoying the beautiful flowers blooming in her yard, she thanked God for them. She prayed for family members. Dawn talked to Jesus about life, big and small things. Instead of being frustrated for an hour, it became an opportunity to enjoy fellowship with God. At 7:00 a.m. she went to her neighbor and got her extra key and let herself back into the house. Prayer had changed the trajectory of her day. She called me later in the day to share what had happened. We talked and laughed together and celebrated all she was learning about praying with her eyes wide open.

How Big Is Too Big?

Nothing is too big for God's power. The one who spoke all creation into existence and sustains all things by his word is entirely capable of meeting any need we face. It is always right to come to our heavenly Father and ask for his help, protection, strength, and healing. He wants to hear our prayers and he delights to answer. This does not mean God will always answer the way we would expect or want. It does mean he is able and we should come and ask with confident faith.

I have found that one area of big prayers that some Christians are reluctant to bring to God is healing prayers. What if I ask in faith and God does not heal? If the prayer is not answered the way I think it should be, is it because I lack faith? Some very sincere followers of Jesus resist coming and asking for God's healing.

I encourage you to always ask of God. Cry out to him in faith and declare your trust. Express that you know God has the power to heal and restore. Dare to ask for God's healing touch. At the same time, place yourself and those you love in the hands of the Sovereign God who is wiser than you are. Declare your faith that God can heal and also your faithfulness to him if he decides not to heal. We don't raise a fist at God and demand healing. We come with humble hearts and ask for God to do what only he can accomplish. We also keep following him and praising him when he heals and when he does not.

Friendship and Healing Prayers

Marce is a close friend who has gone through more surgeries than almost anyone I have ever met. She also has a relentlessly resilient and joyful spirit. She does not complain but places her faith in Jesus each day, walks with him, and prays for healing with faith-filled confidence. We have become friends and prayer partners over the years.

One day I was talking with Marce on the phone. She shared that she had just gotten the report on another CT scan and they had found a spot on her back. We prayed for her. I was getting ready for a second epidural that the doctor had recommended to try to relieve some of the constant pain in my leg and back. She prayed for me. We both asked God for healing—a big prayer. We also both confessed to God that we would love and follow him if we did not experience the healing we desired.

It is hard to put into words how sweet this experience was. Both Marce and I love Jesus. We live and walk in faith . . . even when walking is painful. We rejoice with each other in times of healing or when one of us experiences relief from pain or receives a great report from a doctor. We comfort each other when the pain continues and the future seems uncertain. In all situations we keep praying big prayers with big faith.

My Grace Is Sufficient

I lived with chronic pain for two years. I pressed on and lived life, but pain was a constant uninvited guest every day. I regularly prayed for healing, sometimes through tears. I prayed in faith and trust. I prayed for God's will in my life. Finally, my doctor told me he really believed I needed a surgery that would remove two of the ruptured discs in my neck and replace them with titanium discs that would be set into my vertebrae. I prayed that there would be some way we could afford this surgery. Many others had success with this procedure.

The problem was the surgery needed a couple more years of trial before insurance would cover part of the cost. We would have to pay for the whole surgery in cash and we did not have near enough money.

We kept praying. Over the coming months, a number of things happened. A few friends heard about the need and offered to help with the cost of the surgery. Another friend who works in the medical community helped find ways to reduce some of the costs. My doctor and physical therapist offered to reduce their fees as well. Kevin and I were able to come up with the remaining portion. I had the surgery and it was successful!

Over the next couple of years God opened the door to a series of amazing friendships through my surgery and recovery. We have become good friends with my surgeon and his wife. We have also become like family with the team at the physical therapist's office. I am still there for some other ongoing health challenges. I am so thankful for the excellent care I am receiving through them. My life has been enriched through these relationships more than I could have imagined.

I think of the apostle Paul praying for God to remove his thorn in his flesh (2 Cor. 12:8). God's response was, "My grace is sufficient for you, for my power is made perfect in weakness" (2 Cor. 12:9). I have prayed big prayers for healing in my life and the lives of people I love. There have been times when God's answers were nothing short of miraculous. There have been other times God has said no to my prayer, but he has also unleashed his amazing grace in surprising ways and it is always enough.

The Rest of the Story

While I was speaking at the women's conference in Adelaide, Australia, I decided to tell all the women about how God had answered Alma's "Koala Prayer." It was such a sweet story and I knew it would encourage them to pray about little things and big things in their lives. In the middle of my koala story, a murmur started in part of the room and began to spread like wildfire. Women were whispering, pointing, and giggling. As a communicator, I knew I had lost their attention. The women were no longer looking at me . . . they were all looking out a large window just behind me.

I turned around to see what had grabbed their attention. There on the branch of a eucalyptus tree was a very large, very cute, eyes-wide-open koala who had positioned himself right behind and above my head as I was telling my story. The koala was staring right into the room and looking at the women and me.

Before you knew it, women were out of their seats, they had cameras out, they were delighting and rejoicing in this wonderful moment. Some of them had rarely seen a koala and never one this big and wide-awake in the middle of the day (very unusual for koalas to be seen in the daytime with eyes wide open). We all had a sense that this was another answer to a prayer about a small thing. God was giving us a sweet reminder that he answers prayers, both big and small.

Your Prayer Journey

Think about some small thing that just might bring a blessing to another person. Begin praying about it. Keep lifting it up and asking for God to surprise, bless, and show his love to them. Try texting or emailing a prayer to someone in your life. I don't mean send them a text saying, "I will pray for you" (although that is good to do at times too). Instead, type a prayer and send it. I have a dear friend, Nancy, who will often pray Scripture. When we can't get together to pray, Nancy will send text messages with a prayer or a Scripture prayer. Here is a recent text she sent me:

> **Nancy**
> Hi Sherry, praying for you . . . "Therefore I have hope. The Lord's loving kindnesses indeed never cease, for His compassions never fail. They are new every morning; great is Your faithfulness." "The Lord is my portion." Says my soul, "Therefore I have hope in Him" Lamentations 3:21–24.

Take time this week and text or email a prayer to someone in your life.

Sixteen

Something Happens Every Time You Pray

We can do nothing without prayer. All things can be done
by importunate prayer. It surmounts or removes all obstacles,
overcomes every resisting force and gains its ends in the face
of invincible hindrances.

E. M. BOUNDS

We were on a short-term mission trip in the Netherlands. A team
from our church was partnering with a wonderful congregation,
Crossroads International Church, in Amstelveen. The church
had been setting up and tearing down in a rented facility for
many years. They had grown to be one of the largest congregations in the country. Our team came to lead worship, provide
preaching, help out with all of the setup and teardown, and do
leadership training for two weekends.

On a few of the weekdays, we spent time inviting people
to church and seeking to build relationships with people in

the community and congregation. Our time reaching out to unchurched people seemed to bear very little fruit. The Netherlands is radically post-Christian, and when people heard we were from a church, many simply shut down and walked away.

At the end of each day, Kevin and I would gather our three sons and debrief. One evening we asked our boys, "What did you learn today?" Our middle son, Josh, who was twelve at the time, said, "Something happened every time we prayed." There was confidence in his tone and words.

I was surprised, because I was not feeling as optimistic as he was. Honestly, I was a little concerned that this might end up being a discouraging mission trip experience for the boys. I had focused on the rejection and how most people were not very interested in church or talking about faith. I asked Josh to explain. He went on to recount that all through the day we had prayed and each time God did something. At times it was small and at times it was big, but Josh was right.

Josh went on to explain that when we had car troubles at the start of the day, we prayed and we figured out how to solve the problem. He continued observing that when we went out to invite people to church, most were not interested, but there were a few people who seemed a little interested and, even though only one couple said they might come, there were at least two people who might visit the church on Sunday.

I had missed it, but Josh had not. Something happened every time we prayed. It might not have been what I wanted or expected, but God was clearly present and on the move.

There was spiritual activity, fruitfulness, or some kind of divine intervention each time we prayed. The words of my twelve-year-old son have stuck with me for a decade and a half. His words, "Something happened every time we prayed," encourage me to this day. We may not always see it, but God's power is released and something happens every single time we pray.

Surprising Answers

If we live with confidence that something happens every time we pray, we will learn to recognize and be amazed by God's surprising answers to our daily prayers. But if we expect God to always answer the way we think he should, we will miss the glory and wonder of God's creative responses.

The Bible is full of surprising answers to prayer. When Peter was thrown in prison by the insane whim of King Herod, he would have been praying for release, comfort, and hope in what looked like a hopeless situation. Just a short time earlier, Herod had arrested James (the brother of John) and had him executed (Acts 12:1-2). One of Jesus' closest friends had been martyred. James was in the inner circle of disciples that Jesus invested in and mentored intimately. The other two were John, the brother of James, and Peter. There is no way Peter would have felt safe or assured that he would leave prison alive.

Herod had arrested him and thrown him in jail because he saw that the religious leaders took delight when James was killed. Herod had Peter put under the guard of sixteen soldiers. One fisherman-turned-evangelist needed four squads of soldiers to guard him. Herod's plan was to do a quick trial after the Festival of Unleavened Bread was over and then have Peter killed also. It seemed his death was inevitable (Acts 12:3-4).

There was just one little wrinkle in Herod's plan. The church was earnestly praying for Peter (Acts 12:5). The prayers of God's people were ascending to heaven like incense. God heard. God acted.

Remember, something happens every time we pray. This time, the something that happened was extraordinary. It was more than any of the people could have imagined or dreamed . . . including Peter. It is not that they lacked faith. But what God did was so far beyond their imagination that they would not have had a category for the kind of answer they received.

Peter was imprisoned in a locked cell with sixteen soldiers ready to stop any escape or jailbreak. Two of these soldiers were chained to Peter, one on each side of him. Sentries were at the door. There was no way out. Or so it seemed (Acts 12:6).

God's people were praying and things were about to get very interesting and exciting! The night before Peter was to go on trial, the prayers of God's people were answered in a shocking way. Hours before Peter was to be accused and executed, heaven opened and God showed up.

In a matter of moments, the following things happened in response to the prayers of God's people: An angel appeared and radiated piercing light in the cell where Peter was incarcerated. The angelic being poked Peter and woke him up. He spoke to Peter and told him to get up. Peter's chains just fell off his wrists. The angel told Peter to get dressed and follow him out of the jail. They walked past all the guards without being noticed. The iron gate swung open on its own accord. Peter followed the angel all the way out of the prison. Then the angel disappeared!

I would say something happened when God's people prayed. Miracle after miracle unfolded. It was so staggering that Peter thought he was having a dream and did not even think it was real. When the angel finally vanished and Peter realized he was free, he finally got it. Something happens when God's people pray . . . often more than we are prepared for.

When Peter came to the house where God's people were praying, they did not believe it was possible that he was free and at the door. Even though they were praying, they were stunned and had to be convinced that Peter was there and alive (Acts 12:12–17).

When we read a story like this, we might get excited and assume that every time we pray, the answer is a series of astounding miracles that lead to complete and immediate deliverance. This would be nice, but it is not what the Bible teaches. Something happens every time we pray, but things don't always play out like we might expect.

Stop and think about another great biblical leader who was faith-filled and a man of prayer. The apostle Paul served Jesus with passion and total surrender. Over his years of ministry he faced great hardships, persecution, physical beatings, loneliness, rejection, and much more (2 Cor. 12:1–10). At one point, in utter honesty and transparency, Paul wrote about his struggle with what he called his "thorn in the flesh." After receiving "these surpassingly great revelations," he explained, "in order to keep me from becoming conceited, I was given a thorn in my flesh, a messenger of Satan, to torment me. Three times I pleaded with the Lord to take it away from me" (2 Cor. 12:7–8).

We don't know exactly what Paul's "thorn in the flesh" was, but it was so bad that he cried out to God, over and over, for deliverance and for it to be removed. We might expect God to do a miracle and answer by taking it away. After reading about Peter's shocking release from prison with an angelic guide, we might suppose that God would remove the thorn immediately.

This is not what happened.

We know that something happens every time we pray. God always hears. He loves his children. He is all-powerful. So, what did God do? What was the answer to Paul's heartfelt prayer? Are you ready? Here it is. God says, "My grace is sufficient for you, for my power is made perfect in weakness" (2 Cor. 12:9). No angel. No shackles falling off or thorns being removed. No immediate deliverance and spontaneous songs of praise for an undeniable miracle.

Instead, God promises grace. God offers Paul power to make it through the torment of his thorn in the flesh. The thorn will stay, but so will grace. In this moment God says, "Let my presence and power be enough for you."

Paul's prayers were answered, but in a way very different than he expected. He wanted the thorn gone. God said, "No." The Lord of creation knew that what Paul needed was power in weakness and grace in the pain of life.

Something happens every time you pray. For Peter, it was more than he expected. For Paul, the answer was different than he wanted, but exactly what he needed. As we walk through life, praying with our eyes and lives wide open, praying for people and with people, praying for small things and big things, we can be assured that something will happen every time we pray. We can also be certain that God's answers will rarely look exactly like what we imagine or expect.

God Gets the Glory

On August 10, 2015, Kevin and I met with two executives from Baker Publishing to talk about this book. Jack Kuhatschek and Rod Jansen are both passionate followers of Jesus and fantastic leaders in the Christian publishing world. We have known Jack for over two decades and consider him not only a partner in publishing but a close personal friend.

While we talked and waited for our server to bring our meals, Jack asked, with bold frankness, "How is this book about prayer going to be different than all the other prayer books out there?" I shared about the vision of helping people learn to pray all through their day. I introduced the idea of making praying with eyes wide open a normal part of prayer. Jack decided to challenge me with a real situation in his own life and why my proposed book on prayer would be a good one for him to read. He said, "Well, I have been trying to sell my house for over three months now and we have prayed. The truth is, we are not getting many calls from people who even want to look at the house, and those who look at it are not interested."

I responded like I do to people all the time. I said, "Well, let's pray right now. We don't need to close our eyes." Then I just started praying. It was short and to the point. I humbly asked God to bring a buyer and to help Jack and Sandy sell their house so they could make a move to their new home in Florida where they would begin their retirement years. I asked for patience if the timing was going to be longer than they had planned. I prayed that God would do this for his own glory.

The rest of the people at the table agreed, with eyes wide open. Then our food came and we ate. I told Jack I would continue to pray for the sale of their home. When I got in the car to drive away from our meeting, I prayed again.

Only a few hours later that same afternoon, Jack got a call from his realtor telling him that two different parties wanted to look at the house. Jack told my husband, in kind of a kidding way, that if one of those buyers ended up purchasing the house, he would personally endorse the book. I later received this email:

Sherry,

Thanks so much for your prayers! We put our home on the market in late April and then went through a series of price reductions over the next few months. During that time we had very few showings and only two low offers. We had lunch with you and Kevin on August 10th, and you offered to pray for us. That afternoon I told you that our realtor contacted us and asked if they could have two showings that day (after your prayer). One of the couples who looked at the house that day ended up buying it!

Jack

I was so happy for Jack and Sandy. I did not see this as surprising or shocking. Something happens every time we pray, and this was the way God decided to answer that specific prayer. I was confident that God was being glorified through this answered prayer.

Here is a portion of the email I received from Jack on September 25:

Sherry and Kevin,

We closed on our home today—praise God! We can trace the buyers back to the very day you offered to pray for us at Chili's, which is so encouraging to us.

Those words, "Praise God!" jumped out at me. That is what it is all about, the glory of God. When we pray, trusting in faith, God gets the glory when he answers our prayers.

One wonderful personal ending to this story is that I have had the privilege to have Jack be the acquiring editor of this book, even though he has officially retired. Honestly, an answer to one of my prayers. It was Jack who, so many years earlier, was the first person to encourage me to write a book.

Prayers like Incense

Some years ago Kevin and I were speaking for a group of leaders at a denominational gathering in Cleveland, Tennessee. We were going to be with this group for an extended amount of time over a few days, so we began by introducing ourselves and sharing one fact about ourselves. As one gentle and sweet woman opened up, she shared she had just learned she had cancer. My heart ached for her and I wanted to pray. It seemed only right to stop and pause and pray for her. So I asked the whole group if we might pray for this dear woman, thinking I would lead in a short prayer.

What happened next was surprising, and glorious. As I began to pray, every person in the room also prayed, but not silently. They all lifted their voices with passion and volume. In a matter of seconds I could hardly hear my own voice. What I learned later was that people from their church tradition would normally all pray out loud at the same time. At that moment, I kept praying, but I also wondered, how will they know when we are done? After a few minutes of unified expressive prayer, the volume went down and I said, "Amen!"

In the coming days we prayed together many more times. I quickly got used to all the voices being lifted up at the same time. In private, Kevin made a comment to me about how hearing the prayers of many voices lifted at the same time must be a little like what God hears. The Lord of glory hears all of our prayers being lifted in a perpetual concert of praise, confession, lament, and supplication.

I love the picture in the book of Revelation where John writes, "The four living creatures and the twenty-four elders fell down before the Lamb. Each one had a harp and they were holding golden bowls full of incense, which are the prayers of God's people" (5:8). Our prayers float up toward heaven like incense. Tens of thousands, hundreds of thousands, millions of prayers at any given moment ascending to the very throne room of God like sweet incense. What a picture . . . what a spiritual reality!

When we pray through the flow of each day, our heart's cry joins the prayers of God's people around the world. They are lifted up and God hears, he cares, he answers.

Something happens every time you pray. One of the things that happens is that God is glorified.

Keep Praying

Years ago I was overwhelmed with the simple two-word verse, "Pray continually" (1 Thess. 5:17). Now I have learned that this passage is not saying we have to pray every moment of every day, but we are invited to. This is a decision that becomes a lifestyle.

One "something" that is happening every time you pray is exercising your faithfulness to God. In Romans 12:12 the apostle Paul writes, "Be joyful in hope, patient in affliction, faithful in prayer." That is my desire for my life and for yours, "be faithful in prayer." To do this, we will pray in many places and circumstances. This means at times we will need to pray with our eyes wide open. As we do, prayer will become a lifestyle, like breathing. The more we pray, the more we will encounter God, hear from him, be transformed, and give him all the glory and praise that he deserves.

Closing Prayer

God of all power who is present with his children at all times and in all places, teach us to pray in the normal flow of our life. Open our eyes to see the pain of this world and pray for your healing touch. Let us see how you are moving in wonderful and glorious ways to share your love. Help us notice where you are at work and moving and pray for your glory to be revealed. Open our ears to hear your voice and follow your leading. Move our hands to action birthed in prayer. Transform our lives so that we are ever surrendered to your will and ways. Thank you that you hear our prayers, large and small, that you care, that you answer according to your perfect will. Father, Son, and Holy Spirit, we are your children. Teach us, lead us, and remind us each day that if we pray with our eyes wide open, our time with you is limitless. In the powerful name of Jesus, Amen! (Prayed with my eyes wide open!)

Your Prayer Journey

Start a journal of simple prayers of thanks for answered prayers you have experienced. What has God done in response to your prayers or the prayers of people you love? As you identify how God has moved, answered, or shown up, give him thanks for being a God who hears and works on our behalf. You might want to share some of the answered prayers with Christian friends and even with people you love who are not yet followers of Jesus.

Notes

Chapter 2 Pray Continually

1. Jonathan Edwards, Henry Rogers, Sereno Edwards Dwight, and Edward Hickman, *The Works of Jonathan Edwards, A. M.* (London: Ball, Arnold, and Co., 1840), 116.
2. John Piper, *God's Passion for His Glory: Living the Vision of Jonathan Edwards* (Wheaton: Crossway, 1998), 43.

Chapter 4 Power in Prayer

1. Dallas Willard, session at the National Pastors' Conference.
2. Samuel Chadwick, in Nick Harrison, *Magnificent Prayer* (Grand Rapids: Zondervan, 2001), 365.

Chapter 9 The Father Is Fond of You

1. Brennan Manning, *Abba's Child: The Cry of the Heart for Intimate Belonging* (Colorado Springs: NavPress, 1994), 64.
2. A. W. Tozer, *The Knowledge of the Holy* (New York: HarperOne, 1978), 1.

Chapter 10 Honest to God

1. Dietrich Bonhoeffer, *Psalms: The Prayer Book of the Bible* (Minneapolis: Augsburg Fortress, 1970).
2. This structure is taken from Bernhard W. Anderson with Steven Bishop, *Out of the Depths: The Psalms Speak to Us Today* (Philadelphia: Westminster Press, 1983), 76–77.
3. Max Lucado, *You'll Get Through It* (Nashville: Thomas Nelson, 2013), 29.

Chapter 11 Warfare Prayers

1. Klyne Snodgrass, *NIV Application Commentary on Ephesians* (Grand Rapids: Zondervan, 1996), 344.

Chapter 13 Praying for Others

1. Max Lucado, *Before Amen: The Power of a Simple Prayer* (Nashville: Thomas Nelson, 2014), 75.
2. Charles Stanley, *Handle with Prayer* (Wheaton: Victor Books, 1986), 95.

Chapter 14 Praying with Others

1. A. W. Tozer, *Tozer on the Almighty God: A 365-Day Devotional* (Chicago: Moody, 2004), Jan. 11.

Chapter 15 Praying for the Little and Big Things of Life

1. C. S. Lewis, *The Weight of Glory* (San Francisco: Harper One, 1949; rev. 1980), 26.
2. Ron Dykstra, *Clean Jokes, Inspirational Stories, and More: A Collection by Ron Dykstra* (Oklahoma: Tate Publishing & Enterprises, 2009), 26–27.

Sherry Harney is an author and speaker who serves as the leadership development director at Shoreline Community Church in Monterey, California. She is also the cofounder of Organic Outreach International, a ministry that trains church and movement leaders to mobilize their members to go into their communities and the world to share the good news of Jesus. For over two decades, Sherry has spoken for local, national, and international groups and events. She focuses on prayer, spiritual formation, leadership, and Organic Outreach. She and her husband, Kevin, have coauthored books and have partnered in writing small group study guides with writers such as Ann Voskamp, Max Lucado, Nabeel Qureshi, Bill Hybels, John Ortberg, Mark Batterson, Christine Caine, Gary Thomas, and Dallas Willard.

OrganicOutreach

INTERNATIONAL

Connect with Sherry and Kevin!

Kevin and Sherry Harney are cofounders of Organic Outreach International, a ministry that trains church and movement leaders to mobilize people to go into their community and world and naturally share the good news of Jesus Christ.

WWW.ORGANICOUTREACH.ORG

ShorelineMonterey   @ShorelineChurch